BARRY ROSE'S
ANECDOTAGE

Printed by: EntaPrint Ltd, Cranleigh, Surrey

BARRY ROSE'S

ANECDOTAGE

Myself, against the backcloth of some of the 54 annual volumes of the J.P. which formed the basis of my professional life.

ISBN 1 870234 05 7

Published by
Countrywise Press Limited
East Row, Little London,
Chichester, England

Whereas my contemporaries occupied their time (war service permitting, for I am talking of 1943) on sensible activities such as various forms of sport, I was working (literally) seven days a week. Thus, I am tempted to use the sub-title, "An Account of an Unspent Youth".

However, I was employed by the world's oldest weekly law journal; the war was at its height; I was Grade 4 and in receipt of a letter (cyclo-styled) from Mr Ernest Bevin, the Minister of Labour imploring me to carry on working, despite my health, for as long as I could. Well, neither he nor I could have visualised that I would remain at the same desk doing the same job for the next 54 years.

Well, not quite the same: I bought the journal from Butterworths (then as now the largest law publishers in the Commonwealth) and sold it back to them, plus accretions (11 other journals) and started a book imprint which has produced some hundreds of titles - I still retain the imprint.

In the meantime, I became deeply involved in local politics and local affairs generally: here, I have tried to provide details to complete some items which at the time excited some public interest and which may be found in the Appendices - I hope I have not descended into pomposity, but have attempted to close the ledgers.

My account of snippets of conversations - I hope I have not misquoted anyone; naturally, at all times, I have tried to be accurate but if I have not succeeded, I apologise in advance to the person(s) concerned.

My thanks are due to my wife Jean, whose continuing contribution to public life by far outshines my own, and whose personal support over the past 40 years (including being my chauffeuse!), is something difficult for me to adequately repay. And my thanks to Mrs Fleet, who has been asked to perform incredible feats on her computer to cope with the alterations, additions and deletions. Also to Terence Pickering, for his professional skills with the camera and for his friendship at particular times, such as that Old Bexley Election campaign.

Barry Rose
August 2003

"Barry Rose's Anecdotage" is, basically, a bedside book. The following is a guide (in page order) to some of its principal contents:

Cricket is a team sport; there is some ground for believing that it first burst upon the scene in West Sussex, although Hampshire has a pretty strong claim to its origins, too. Well, I am about to retell a story which my gentle reader will regard with disbelief - because it is the story how, despite it being a team game, one man was able to win the match. And that one man was me. Indisputably I won it single-handed - but let the story tell its own tale.

* * * * *

War had just reached the stage where Dunkirk was now behind us and the country was mobilized - mobilized, so that it was always difficult for teams to be made up, and in 1942 when the captain of the village team said in the bar of the *Lamb Inn* at Pagham that he was one man short for tomorrow's game, it was no great surprise to anyone. The worthy landlord (doubtless having just read a letter from me in a daily paper protesting at cricket pitches being ploughed up whereas all sorts of other meadows were left intact) said that, "Well, of course, there's Barry Rose" or something to this effect. Now I know he should not have said this, but he did - and an invitation was extended to me to report in my whites at 2 p.m. the following day. What he did not tell the skipper (mainly I suspect because he did not know) was the existence of a recently acquired kitten which had taken a liking to me - a liking, if I may say so, which was fully reciprocated. Alas, no one in those distant days knew anything about allergies, but the cat's fur induced in me a most terrible form of asthma which stayed with me until I was 42; of course, I should have turned down the invitation - but cricket was then the love of my life, and before the kitten had been acquired, I think it would be fair to say that I had a certain aptitude.

But I turned up, complete with my asthma, but without any

time in the nets, and was put in No. 6, and was out first ball.

To field, when we were doing rather well definitely in a winning position so far as anything in cricket can be certain, the skipper invited me to bowl. That was the second mistake he made that day - the other having invited me to play in the first place. But a chap can only do what he's told to do; he has unquestioningly to obey the orders of his skipper, so we set a fast field and I began a run up of the length favoured by, say, a Larwood or a Bowes or a Farnes - for we are speaking of that sort of era - but long before I reached the crease my breath gave out. It was in the days of the eight ball over, and what with no balls and wides, the home side scored off that one over, 36 runs; they couldn't believe their luck. The next over, fielding slip, I was still so out of breath that I put down two catches of incredible simplicity.

I told them at the time - that when the history of the summer game comes to be written, the historic match between Priory Park and Pagham will live ever more - how one man won the game single-handed for the other side.

For the life of me, I can't figure out why - but they never asked me to play for them again.

Yet to be fair, the president, who was a member of the MCC, asked me if I'd care to be a member, presumably thinking I would do less harm that way, "But Rose, I must warn you, there's a waiting time of four years." To a young man, four years seemed a lifetime; to a young man with asthma, it seemed I would never make it; stupidly, I turned down the offer, and by the time I had changed my mind, the waiting time had been extended to eight years. I am told it is now, in 2003, 18 years.

* * * * *

The Minister for War, Anthony Eden, announced in May 1940, to a welcoming nation the formation of Local Defence Volunteers. It was to be a citizen force and I think the basic idea was that we should repel the enemy with the aid of anything that came to hand, such as pitchforks and pikes. Also, of course, .22 rifles and such other guns as we might possess. Bearing in mind we had just lost most of the equipment of the British Expeditionary Force in the events leading to Dunkirk, this seemed reasonable enough, and I recall that I registered No. 54 in Sussex at the local Police Station, which of course was caught on the hop by the Eden announcement and completely unable to cope with the huge number of people who wanted to do something, anything, to fight for their homes and country.

My period with the LDV (subsequently transformed into the Home Guard) was short, but two incidents stick in my mind. The first concerned a Captain Jones (his real name, and not Corporal Jones, as in *Dad's Army*), who gave us a lecture on first aid. He had served (no doubt with distinction) in the Boer War, and had then been promoted from the ranks to Captain in the first World War. He had been gassed, and I remember the poor chap particularly for the cough he had at all times, as a legacy of the gas. He was giving instructions on the course to follow if wounded or if a comrade was bleeding from a bullet wound - no doubt his instruction was sound, but I did not hear anything from the moment he mentioned the word "blood". I had fainted.

I was then transferred to Pagham Home Guard, and was on guard duty at the approaches to Pagham Harbour - a place which was subsequently to figure large in my early life. The purpose was to guard the Harbour, for two hours before sunset, and for two hours before sunrise. By this time, we had some Canadian .303 Ross rifles, and also each had five very precious rounds of ammunition. Many nights we could see the terrible fires caused by bombing raids at Portsmouth, and also our anti-aircraft fire giving a savage beauty to the scene - but we never saw a plane ourselves (not when I was on duty, anyway). Yet the funny thing was that the German radio would broadcast often - through the mouth of "Lord Haw-Haw", William Joyce, that German bombers had bombed Pagham Harbour the previous night. Well, if so, we neither saw nor heard them - again, not when I was on duty, anyway.

* * * * *

However, looking at it from the point of view of someone who has always been interested in war as an armchair strategist, it made a lot of sense. The Harbour had not been used as such since the seventeenth century when it became silted up (although since there is a fairly modern customs house at Sidlesham at the neck of the harbour, maybe it was used for rather more than the sort of coal-barge landings which apparently were fairly common). Anyway, under a Private Act of Parliament in the 1880s, its entrance had been stopped up and the drained 800-odd acres had been used for farming, until a wild night on Easter Friday, 1910, when the sea broke through and reclaimed it. It is still possible to see the remains of bridges over the rifes, etc., even at this remove in time, but the point I am making is that (when our chaps were expecting a landing in the Dover/Margate area) a landing at Pagham Harbour where there was little water, no cliffs to climb, and therefore a fairly easy landing could have been expected, and a German force could have got round Portsmouth, gained control of the Port in the same way as the Japanese captured Singapore (ie, when our guns and forces were facing the wrong way) and have more or less a clear run to London while our forces were in Kent waiting for a landing in the

Dover area. But the Pagham Home Guard was there to stop them, *and* we each had five rounds of ammunition. I don't think this is classified now, so I can mention it.

But alas, I was not there to share in the glory for much longer; everyone had to work during the daytime, apart, that is, from those who were too old to work, and therefore sleep was a very valuable commodity - but the sound of my wheezing prevented everyone else from getting any sleep. I was therefore asked to resign. The humiliation, the shame of it all - being asked to resign from the Home Guard! But at least, so far as I know, it must have been an unusual reason, almost unique in the annals of the Defence of Britain. Yes, I did my stuff, in standing down.

* * * * *

I have mentioned the bombing of Portsmouth, and after a very heavy raid, one of the leading departmental stores in the city was gutted. Those days after the War when we were both not otherwise engaged, I would have luncheon with Alderman Tozer, a member of Chichester City council and the proprietor of the multiple store called Morants which had been the Portsmouth store destroyed. He told me that the day following the raid, which had destroyed his shop, he had come to Chichester and taken over the premises which now form part of the Army and Navy Stores in West Street, using what stock he could salvage from Portsmouth and of course, with a permit to replace War-damaged stock. The speed and smoothness with which the whole operation was carried out was quite astonishing. He made a remark, however, in a completely different context which has always remained with me. "When I choose a new lady member of staff, I watch her as she walks across the room, and then I chat to her." I make the decision whether or not I will

5

employ her on the basis, 'Would I like to take her out to dinner?' Naturally, I would never invite her - but whether I think I would *like* to, governs my decision." Somehow I don't think he would be happy in today's employment law climate.

* * * * *

West Dean House was owned by an eccentric multi-millionaire called Edward James - he variously described himself as the son of Edward VII, and his mother as the daughter of the King. That was the least of his eccentricities - his putative father had amassed his very substantial fortune by providing the rails upon which the American railway system had been built, and his acquisition of the house ultimately but without the surrounding 1,500 acres came into the leased possession of Stanley Shaw Bond, the proprietor of Butterworths (my employers). The son of James had married Tilly Losch, the 'notorious' singer, dancer and everything merry and bright. She found the house dismal, and left a heartbroken Edward who declared he would never again enter it. Bond took over as tenant, and subsequently (as a result of the outbreak of War) made it the offices (and in effect the dormitories) for some of his staff. Which was where I came in, although I was a day boy. Before the War actually broke out, James went to live in Mexico, leaving behind a treasure house of modern art (Picassos by the dozen, etc.) which subsequently - on fire watching duty (I was there every Saturday from 8.30 a.m.to 8.30 p.m. to fire guard) although no one was allowed to even glimpse the works of art which were kept in a room very securely locked.

I was frequently the only member of the firm present (sometimes I was joined by others, and including a girl (Barbara Bech) who subsequently became the wife of a chap who was a very dear friend of mine - Simon Partridge - but such delightful occasions were alas all too rare). I was of course utterly useless as I did not know how to operate a fire-bucket having no mechanical skills whatever even had I been shown where the equipment was. But still, the powers that be decided that just as I was useless in the Home Guard, I could make myself just as useless as a firewatcher. This was my war-work, for which, incidentally, I was paid a handsome sum by a grateful State - some 3s 6d per diem I seem to recall.

But obviously the grateful State could not allow me to starve, so it brought in a staff to keep me fed - thus, I would often sit alone in a vast baronial hall for luncheon, and then (generally) be joined for dinner by a few members of the firm returning from shopping expeditions in the neighbouring cities, Portsmouth and Brighton and Chichester, before I departed homewards at 8.30 p.m. But the staffing of the house was much the same as it had been prior to the first World War, and the personnel happily still around. It was of course most interesting to talk to them and hear tell of the monarchs who had stayed there over the years, such as Alfonso of Spain, of the old King Edward VII and of the house parties held there. James himself seemed to be held in a sort of awed contempt - these worthy people, of course, had no conception of why a man with so much to make his life comfortable in West Dean House, should depart for the jungles of Mexico to build some sort of mock village which, after the jungle had swallowed it, as it probably has by now, will have archeologists scratching their heads a thousand years hence wondering as to its meaning.

Tales about him abounded - for example, he once (on his return to England and despite his earlier declaration about never setting foot in West Dean House after Tilly Losch had left him) went into the carpenters' shop and went down the line of craftsmen there: he went to one and said, for no reason that anyone could fathom, "You're fired." "Pardon, Sir," said the man, cupping his hand over his ear. "You're fired," said James again, "Sorry, Sir," said the man, "I can't hear you; I'm deaf." James apparently tried again, and then said, breaking away in disgust, "Oh - forget it," and continued his inspection.

* * * * *

At the end of the War, Butterworths moved back to London - but I politely declined to go with them, so instead it was agreed that I could stay to run the *Justice of the Peace* and *Local Government Review* (always known as the *J.P.*) (with my own tiny staff) in Chichester.

I shared my office building with the *Chichester Observer*, which was owned by R.J. Acford Ltd. Acfords owned a printing works which printed the *J.P.* and various other periodicals owned by Butterworths, such as the *All England Law Reports*. The building itself had been built (or rather "finished") in 1630, and I was told it was the oldest industrial building in the country still in use. Originally, it had been a needle factory, then a brewery, and finally a printers' and newspaper office.

My relations were very cordial with the *Chichester Observer* people, and because of my "experience" in the libel case brought by the *Daily Mirror* against the *J.P. (post)*. I was considered an expert in libel law by the editor (who was also effectively the owner of the paper) and once or twice she sent reporters to me for my opinion (the Bar Council or the Law Society need not become agitated - it was for no fee!). Of course, most of the more dedicated reporters wished to get away to the glittering lights of Fleet Street - since dispersed all over London - and a few succeeded, including one girl, Jan Reid.

Years later we met by coincidence in a dentist's waiting room, and she told me the following: On her first day with the *Daily Mail*, she was told to interview the winner of one of their competitions, on what it was like to win a Rolls Royce or whatever it was. She was told the winner was on holiday in Swi, in Yugoslavia, and she was told to collect her passport, and some money from the cashier, and be on her way. This was the first day for her in Fleet Street.

She duly arrived at Swi - the place had but one hotel, and the local Police seemed to be interested in her mission - but of the winner and his wife in this small town in the Balkans, there was no sign. She phoned the *Daily Mail*, and she was told to keep searching as the two winners were known to be there. The Police became even more suspicious when she made repeated inquiries at the Police Station, the hospital and every other likely and unlikely place. She decided that there was no point in staying, so two days later she returned to England. Immediately she reported back with no story, she was angrily told to return, so she went back and the Police at Swi were even more suspicious; of the missing couple there was still no sign.

Then the London Office phoned her and instructed her to return at once. She got back, fearing that her career at the *Mail* was about to be cut short; however, no word was said and she was sent on some other assignment. Later, she discovered that the couple had been on holiday in SW1 - London, SW1, not Swi in Jugoslavia. No one ever said anything to her about that at all. The best stories never get printed.

* * * * *

I once asked Kingsley Amis whether he used a computer to write his novels. He said he won one as a prize in some literary competition and had used it for a month or so, but then handed it back as he could not get on with it all.

When a substantial minority of shares in Butterworths (then a privately owned company) had to be sold to meet the death duties of the former proprietor, S.S. Bond, a city solicitor, Hugh Quennell, was selected to represent the minority interest thereby created. I have mentioned elsewhere the libel action brought by the *Daily Mirror* against the *J.P.*; and although at that time Butterworths did not own the *J.P.*, Quennell took the matter out of Emery's hands (he being the representative as managing director of the owner of the *J.P. Ltd*). And decided who should act for us (Valentine Holmes, KC led - incidentally, an acquaintance of my father's), and when the case had been won, wrote a triumphant piece intended to be published in the *J.P.* crowing over the victory. It fell to my (and very apprehensive) lot to refuse to publish. [It was filled with childish flamboyant phrases such as "the *Daily Mirror* can now go back into the gutter where it belongs".]

I wanted to publish a short dignified piece appropriate to the journal - in the end, we published nothing. Perhaps it was as well - as in the passage of years the *Daily Mirror* (through its holding company) came to own the *J.P.* (and from whom I was subsequently to acquire it). On another occasion, Quennell thought he had me, as the result of a mistake in a headline to an article - apparently he was having dinner the previous night with Hartley Shawcross, the Attorney-General, who he said had ribbed him about the error. Thirsting for my blood, the following morning (apparently) I was due to be fired - but then it was discovered that I was on holiday in Yorkshire. It was represented to me that it was appreciated that I had to have holidays, but really, this sort of thing must not happen again: Mr. Quennell did not like being made to look a fool especially to the Attorney-General. Thus it was that I ceased to take holidays, but took instead time off in lieu by becoming a member of various local authorities and involving myself ever more deeply in the political and public service, coming back for press day even during my honeymoon. I have little doubt that my own arrangements over time 'in lieu' and the reason for it, was long forgotten; but I was determined that no one would be in a position to ever accuse me of taking time off for all my political activities, and to be fair, no one did. It certainly was not fair on my wife and daughter who never had a holiday with me - although I console myself we were living in a holiday environment, close to the sea and they went away on their own.

* * * * *

On a semi-private occasion more than 50 years ago, I heard Enoch Powell (not then an M.P.) express the view that the difference between Conservatism and Socialism was that a Conservative believed that Utopia was to be found in lessons of the past, and a Socialist believed it was to be found, undefined, somewhere in the future. I have still to read, or hear, a better reason expressed in a phrase, as to why one should remain a Conservative.

* * * * *

Although "my" famous libel action had originated at West Dean, it saw its completion in what were to become my new offices for almost 20 years in Chichester, and not a day passed without me being terrified of fire breaking out - my offices were furthest away from the wooden staircase that led to the street and to safety. When I say that there was a well under the stairs which was used for scrap paper, and that smoking was rife among the staff, and that I was on the second floor - perhaps my apprehension can be under-stood.

For this reason I was always trying out new methods of escape in the event of an emergency - I recall one, where we were to climb through a window, and abseil down the wall; we never set it up, as all members of the staff regarded it as inherently unsafe and all said they would not use it. I ordered a new contraption which was a sort of collapsible ladder - made of aluminium or lightweight steel - it took about six years (yes, six years) to be delivered, and arrived the very week we moved out - but I do not suppose anyone would have felt inclined to trust themselves to such a flimsy and altogether strange device: apparently you threw it out of the window and it unfurled itself on the way down - I do not recall what was said about the likely fate to befall those pedestrians walking underneath.

I recall also a traveller selling us an "anti-fire" gun, which came with five large cartridges. Apparently you fired it over the fire that was breaking out and a cloud of chemicals was ejected which destroyed the fire by depriving it of oxygen. So much for the theory. I thought we should have some staff training on how this should be used - but of course there was no fire and I thought the chemicals might be dangerous in a closed environment - so we went outside bearing this strange looking gun. As we had no grounds, we had to use the street of Little London itself; I made sure it was loaded and then, following instructions, aimed it at the heart of an imaginary fire on the ground at my feet. I pulled the trigger. Nothing happened. I increased the pressure and pulled it again; still nothing happened. I lifted it in order to see what was wrong with it when ... whoosh, and white chemical powder streamed up Little London to the other side of an adjoining street. I imagine those who found this stuff getting into their eyes and nose and mouth hardly found it amusing, and when I saw a uniformed policeman approaching through the cloud it was plainly time to take our leave.

Those offices - ah yes, they should have been kept and they would have lasted for another three hundred years - the walls were so stout and the oak timbers (by legend, from ships that had fought the Armada, and brought from Portsmouth) that had been used throughout its construction would have taken care of the years. But there were disadvantages. When I first moved in, the floor of my office sagged towards the centre - if say, one dropped a pen, it would roll to the other side of the room - I found myself sitting at one level, working on another and writing at a third, so plainly something had to be done. I got the builders to construct a platform - inevitably called a throne - upon which my desk, chairs, etc., could stand without a bias either to the left or the right.

It is true that my body was no longer twisted into contortions but there were certain disadvantages in having a two-inch high platform (in some places I suspect it was three inches) because although I was aware it was there, some of my visitors were not.

I recall one such person in particular. Evan T. Davies, C.B.E., was a former Director of Education for West Sussex. Without doubt, he did a tremendous amount for the county, and on retirement he decided to continue the good work by becoming a member of it. Now as we all know, it is not always a popular move to make - previous officers know too much of the inner workings; new chief officers resent rather the presence of their predecessors (poachers turned gamekeepers is how it is usually described) - so, Evan, much to his disappointment, was never put on the education committee. Thus, he never really had enough to do.

He was, however, a barrister, and thought he would eke out retirement time by doing a little work for us - digesting cases. So, when he came to see me in my offices, I rose from my seat on the platform, made eye contact, and extended my hand in greeting. He, for his part, extended his hand and made eye contact with me -

unfortunately, however, by doing so, tripped on the platform and fell into the rather sharp corner of my desk which was on the platform. It badly winded him, and he then backed to sit down on the visitor's chair. It was a "utility" chair, bought at the end of the War, and he was a big man - as a result of being winded, he sat down heavily and it collapsed.

There are those who say that Evan was never the same man again (I believe he had to have an operation about a week or fortnight later) but he never seemed to hold it against me. He regaled me with many stories of an era when I was not a member of the county council - such as the chap who was, for 16 years, yes, 16 years! a member of the Local Education Authority and who asked at one meeting, "Can someone tell me what the initials LEA stand for?" Or the chap (whom I knew well and would say this was absolutely true from my own observation of his character) who wanted for his own ambitious reasons to become chairman of the education committee, so he persuaded some of his cronies to speak in a low voice so that the elected chairman had to say, after a time, "I must be going deaf; I had better resign."

But we are getting away from my office. As I have said, we were as a company owned by Butterworths, but were about 60 miles away, so did not see much of them. One day, I got a message that the chairman himself (the Earl of Rothes, no less) was to pay us a visit. Now I had as my assistant at that time a lovely man, Bill Bray. He was, during the War, a Wing Commander, but unfortunately had contracted TB. He came to me partly to augment his pension, and partly to use his brain. The impending arrival of the chairman of the company stung him into action: at a time when it was possible to have office boys, our young man was put to the clean-up Bill Bray thought the offices needed - by the time the work was completed, the noble Earl could have eaten a meal off the floor. But I don't suppose he would have wanted to.

Things, however, never seem to turn out as expected. He came, accompanied by the managing director of Butterworths, Emery, who seemed excessively nervous in case I said the wrong thing. I took great care to point out the dangers of the corner of the desk and the risks of impaling himself upon it, and tried not to make eye contact so that he spotted the platform. He sat down, and there is only one thing I recall him saying: "There seems to be a curious smell here."

I said, "The place used to be a brewery; that might account for it." "Ah, yes," he nodded wisely, and then departed. Poor dear Bill Bray - all the work and effort he had put in and it hadn't been noticed, much less commented upon.

When he left me, it was to go as licensee of the "George and Dragon" public house, which then had a gory inn sign of "St George Stabbing the Dragon", so it was known as the "Bucket of Blood". He was also the first Conservative Alderman on the City Council - a great fellow and companion, he once told me that when invalided home, he came by liner from South Africa, which was the liner used by the steward who thrust a pregnant woman out of a porthole after killing her - it was a very sensational case at the time. He was the first man not to hang after the Abolition of Capital Punishment by Parliament.

* * * * *

I find taxi-drivers - especially in London - interesting people to talk to - other than when they are listening to Radio One! Late in 2002, one such driver was telling me that he became a taxi-driver after working in the building industry, where he had been employed by contractors on various public buildings including the Bank of England. Once at the Bank, one operative had gestured towards some gold being moved, and said, 'It's all one way: it always goes to Frankfurt, and nothing ever comes back.' Now *that* is basic economics! I wonder if he was right.

* * * * *

He was small in stature, about 5'0½" in height, and never once did I see him when he looked - in his striped trousers, black jacket and waistcoat, other than immaculately dressed. I believe I am right in my memory saying that he wore spats - a rarity even in the 1940s. Of course, he always wore a stiff white winged collar. I would say he was about 75 when I first knew him in 1946.

He would come into my office about once a month, with his latest offering - the articles were first class, and I was pleased, generally, to accept them. His main source of income came from work he performed for a series of law reports then produced in Chichester - proof reading, sub-editing and so on. One day he came into my office in a highly agitated state and burst out, "I cannot have your trust a minute longer. I know you believe I am a solicitor - but I am not - I was struck off and have been to prison."

Poor dear man. I heard his story (I must emphasize it was *his* story) and it was obvious that here was no man using thousands of pounds of other people's money: the total amount involved was about £500 from the sale of two houses, which he said he had every intention of repaying (of course, you will say, they all say that) - of course it is wrong to borrow money from someone else without that person's consent, and there can be absolutely no argument or excuse about that. It was quite obvious to me, however, that his almost fanatical belief in his particular branch of the Christian religion and the free legal aid service he appeared to operate (it was before the introduction of Legal Aid on a national basis) by not sending out bills to those he felt could not afford to pay them, was responsible for what went wrong. He had been sentenced to 12 months at Winchester in, I believe, 1940, and immediately had a nervous breakdown. After a spell in the prison hospital, he was put to work in the prison library - and served, he said bitterly, every day of the sentence with no remission (under the then Prison Rules, apparently a period in hospital did not count as a part of the sentence for the purpose of calculation of remission).

Well, after this somewhat dramatic disclosure, we continued as before, but then the law reports series (not the *Justice of the Peace Reports*) upon whom he depended for his main source of income, had a change of editor who fired him; the editor, perhaps I should add, also fired everyone else employed by the series, except one.

The Clerk to the Justices for Chichester, Bill Booker, duly alerted me to the position, and said somehow we had to help. He undertook to speak to a local firm of solicitors; yes, they would take him on as a clerk, but of course, as he had been struck off, the consent of the Law Society had to be obtained first. The appropriate sub-committee had just met, and would not be meeting for another three months.

Quite by chance, I met him just as I was about to enter my then favourite watering hole in Chichester; it specialized in serving the farming community so it was close to the then thriving market, and I had every reason to suppose that a very full and succulent meal was about to be placed in front of me.

I asked after his health, and in reply he said he had not eaten I think it was for three days. As luck would have it, I was intending to change a cheque in the restaurant and had only a trifling sum in my pocket. He waved my gesture aside to come with me whilst I changed a cheque, and went on his way. So I went off for a most satisfying meal, and he went off hungry. It has haunted me ever since.

Two days later I received a call from a mutual friend who said he was in hospital. I rushed there; the ward sister told me the old man's trouble was starvation. I asked him if there was anything I could get him. He asked for 'an orange'. These were tightly rationed, and generally only released to children and expectant mothers, but of course the chief food executive officer had power to grant a licence for the purchase of an orange for anybody else as he thought fit. I went to see him - but he refused the request. I took my friend a bottle of orange squash, but of course this was rubbish compared with the real orange for which he craved. And so he died. By this time the Welfare State was up and running - and here was a man dying of starvation.

The only postscript I have to make is this: he told me his daughter had been engaged to the man who was later to prosecute him in court, and he, in anticipation of the case, had broken off the engagement. I am sure she was better off without him (she was, incidentally, a strikingly lovely girl). I have often thought of the story and what a Somerset Maughan could have made of it.

* * * * *

A taxi driver (London) told me fairly recently that some time before the War his father had loaded up a barrow with the household effects and had *walked*, pushing the barrow, from Bedford to London, setting out one Friday night. His family (including my taxi driver, then a child) came separately. One used to hear of midnight flits, and one can imagine the surprise and fury of the landlord when he heard about it, without his rent and nothing to distrain on; a classic case of a midnight flit. But *walking* from Bedford to London! ...

A steward in the restaurant car of a train told me that his old mother had wanted one thing all her life - a piece of carpet. "Did she get it?" I asked; he nodded.

Poverty in the 20th century - God knows what it would have been like in the 19th century or earlier.

* * * * *

With a friend I was having a drink when we were joined by the late Lord Killanin, then president of the International Olympic Committee whom I had not previously met and was never to meet again - but the talk automatically turned to Ireland. He said he was that rare breed - a castle Catholic. In Ireland, he had been taught Irish history by the nuns, and then was sent to England where he was taught the exact opposite at Eton.

* * * * *

Before colour became an industry and before it became almost a criminal offence to even discuss it rationally, I remember discussing with one Northern town clerk the problems of his town - and he told me that one of the leaders of the immigrant population (this was, I suppose, about 1965 or thereabouts) had come to discuss the matter of the vote. "Is it not so that we are allowed to vote?" "Yes," said the town clerk, "of course you are." "Why then are we not on the Electoral Register?" The town clerk said he would look into the matter, and in due course the Electoral Registration Officer was called to explain. His explanation that they were all called "Ali" hardly satisfied the town clerk and of course things were remedied forthwith - but it demonstrates how easily problems can arise completely innocent of any evil intention.

It has always seemed to me that the Duchy of Lancaster must be one of the most pleasant public authorities in which to serve - to be separate yet part of, seems, on the surface at any rate - to be getting the best of both worlds. Sir Patrick McColl was the Clerk to the Lieutenancy, the Clerk to the Peace, and the Clerk to the County Council of Lancashire. At least, those were the posts to which he was appointed, so I asked him on one occasion why he called himself "Chief Executive". Now, of course, such a description is common, but in the 1960s decidedly uncommon. "It's perfectly simple, Barry, I get paid more that way." For the uninitiated, the negotiated salary levels of the Clerks were based, broadly, upon the scales fixed in terms of population - obviously, since there was then no such category for chief executives, he could negotiate his own terms. Nowadays, such a title is pretty general in local government as everywhere else.

* * * * *

It entered the folklore of local government that one Local Bill, about 150 years ago, was said to be so long and convoluted, amounting to about 280 clauses, some very technical, that the town clerk was able to insert a clause enabling him to obtain a divorce! I asked a more recent town clerk of the city whether there was any truth in this. Alas, no, but it was a nice story.

* * * * *

Lord Woolton ("Uncle Fred" in War-time mythology, with a background of "Woolton Pie" and other delicacies derived during his War-time period as Minister of Food, and who was - at the end of the War - appointed by Winston Churchill to be Chairman of the

Conservative Party) retired with his new wife (a doctor who had tended him in an illness) intending to live out his remaining years in a country house at Walberton, in the then Chichester constituency. However, the Chichester Association was to deny him his right to retire completely from the scene, and he was invited to become President, an invitation he accepted. On one occasion, Langford-Sainsbury (*q.v.*) and myself went to see him with a present from the Association on a notable anniversary (I think it was a birthday) and he kept us both entranced by speaking in his drawing room, in a relaxed manner, for over an hour, of Winston and of other political leaders of the War-time years. It so happened that at what was, so far as I know, to be his very last meeting in his adopted village, I was asked to be his chairman. His wife pointed out to me his obvious frailty, and said she would be sitting in the front row and would give me a signal when she thought I should bring the proceedings to a close - thus, I confess I do not recall a single word of what he said, as I was so anxiously watching his wife.

* * * * *

I was in the *Nags Head*, a pub in Chichester, awaiting my wife, when a man I did not know invited me to have a drink. I politely declined, explaining that I never drank with strangers. The publican, who was listening, followed me as I moved out to the safety of the restaurant, and told me that the man had been involved as a passenger in a car when the driver unwisely drove onto the railway line and had been killed by an oncoming train; he had been awarded £150,000 in the personal injuries case following it. "I only hope he doesn't spend it all in here," said the publican.

I suppose all the political nonsense in my life started in the run-up to the General Election in 1945, when I had the temerity to write to Conservative Central Office (then occupying a couple of floors in an office building in Victoria Street) offering my services as a parliamentary candidate. I was then coming up to my 22nd birthday; after the Election, with its catastrophic defeat for the Conservatives, I was invited for interview by the Vice-Chairman of the Party, J.P.L. Thomas, M.P., who was in charge of the selection of candidates. I have ever since been appalled by my presumptuousness - but I was duly put on the list of prospective candidates, and some months later, short-listed for Edmonton (then a safe Labour seat).

Looking back, to have put me on the list at all, they must have been pretty hard up for candidates; either that, or completely bereft of their senses. As it was, J.P.L. Thomas (later Viscount Cilcennin) said it might be some time before a seat came up, and suggested in the meantime that I should work for my constituency association. This - depending on how it is regarded - was, for me, either the slippery slope, or the open gate, depending upon how anyone chooses to regard it, for voluntary service, for the following 30-odd years. At the end of it I had been or was involved with some 92 committees (at the last count, and I have probably forgotten one or two) and had attended (rough estimate) well over 4,000 meetings by the time I was 50. (This I know is a small number - my wife over a longer period must have clocked up at least six or seven times that total - if in addition to her political work, her other interests such as church, even Young Republicans when she lived in the USA, honorary speaker for the R.S.P.C.A., etc. are included.)

My own 'constituency' work began with a re-formation meeting of the Bognor Regis Men's Branch Association in 1945, where I knew not a soul, but when the pre-War chairman, having got to the relevant item on the agenda for the election of vice-chairman, asked, "Is Mr. Barry Rose present?" I sheepishly admitted I was, and was thereupon elected. (No Central Office influence here - he was R.J. Acford, the aged proprietor of the firm we used for our printing.)

Thus began my problems, and thus the genesis of this volume. But I lived not in Bognor but in a village on its outskirts (Pagham) where I formed a men's and women's senior branch (using the expedient of the Voting Register, and writing to everyone on it - only about 600 then), being elected chairman and had formed additionally the Bognor Young Conservative branch. Three or four years later, I was elected president at Pagham, and as by that time, I was involved with all sorts of other branches in the constituency, and the Pagham branch was going so successfully there was no compelling need to keep in touch with it on a day-to-day basis.

This was to bring about a problem: a fête was to be held and everyone knew that my weekly press days were sacrosanct - however, on the evening prior to the fete, I got what I can only describe as a frantic call from the chairman, who begged me to entertain the speaker who was coming down from London. She had arranged with someone whose name meant nothing to me (I am not at all sure she even mentioned it) but he had withdrawn his offer to take the speaker and his wife to lunch; she had arranged everything with the hotel - would I please, please, do the entertaining the following day. Well, what else is a president for? "Barry, you're an absolute angel. By the way, the speaker's name is Farey-Jones."

The next day, press day or not, I gravitated to the bar of the hotel, ready to welcome the speaker. Someone I had never met before approached me and asked. "Mr. XXX?" I denied the identification, and he returned to another corner of the bar. In the next half hour, I watched a stream of people come into the hotel bar, have a drink, and then depart. But of our speaker, there was no sign - except I did notice that there was this chap, accompanied by a woman, keeping his eye rather intently upon the door.

As time was getting on, the speaker was late, I decided he would have a problem in having lunch and to be there to perform the opening ceremony at 2.30. At last, therefore, I plucked up courage and approached the chap who earlier had approached me. "Mr. Farey-Jones?" I inquired. "But you said you were not XXX" naming the chap for whom I was in substitution. Oh dear.

We went into luncheon; even now, more than 50 years later, I still remember the tablecloth for being the filthiest I had ever seen, and I have seen nothing like it since. Originally made of linen or cotton, now it was stiffly encrusted with layers of food, dried drink, things that could have been mouse dirts, or just plain honest-to-goodness dirt. And never have I had a meal since to compare with it in terms of vileness. [Of course, in the intervening 50 years, the hotel has changed ownership &c. many times, and today bears no relationship to conditions prevailing then.] But Mr. Farey-Jones affected not to notice such trifles; by this time he was the prospective candidate for Watford; in Savile Row pin-stripe, he looked every inch the sort of parliamentary candidate the Conservative Party needed, and with his elegant and good looking wife, Watford was indeed lucky to have found him.

Now the fête was to be held on a part-field which, before the War, had been a putting green, but which, because of the proximity of the sea, it had been thought necessary to implant with land-mines, in order to stop any German invading force in its tracks. But then, to prevent English people walking over the minefield, and to have the additional benefit of warning the Germans of the places to avoid, it was shielded by barbed wire, rooted to the ground by metal stakes. By 1950, however, Italian Prisoners of War had long since cleared the mines and cut the barbed wire, but evidently no one had said anything about filling in the holes where the mines had lain, or uprooting the stakes to which the remainder of the barbed wire was still attached by their short trailing strands and hidden in the long grass. On that particular day, there was a south-west gale and as we battled against the wind over to the fête, 50 yards or so away from the hotel, so a girl was being carried out on a makeshift stretcher, bloodied and unconscious. The explanation was simple enough: a stall had collapsed as a result of the gale, and the poor girl had been unfortunate enough to be next to it when it tilted over.

As we entered, so the refreshment stall also toppled over, with the loss of much crockery, but our speaker, whatever may have been his private thoughts, carried on. The lady chairman greeted me enthusiastically, "Oh Barry," she said, "You've been an angel." Now remember that word, which had not occurred previously - not "jolly good sort", "splendid fellow", or anything like that might have been appropriate to 1950 usage, but "angel".

Modestly, I suppose I smiled, and said it was nothing, really; that my task was now over, and I could get back to my office with no further delay. But no. "Barry," she continued, "please, please, please stay to introduce the speaker. It's one of those things you do so well." So what is a president for, I thought. "Oh Barry, you are an angel." There was that word again.

The speech that Mr. Farey-Jones was about to make was to be from the deck of a farm cart lent by a farmer member of the committee and had already been fitted out with a table, microphone, three chairs (and probably a union flag). But before we were to get there, much was to happen.

Although all visual trace of the land-mines had been removed, the holes in which they had lain were still there, hidden by grass, and Mrs. Farey-Jones duly trod in one, badly ricking her ankle and laddering her couponed stockings in the process. Our worthy speaker, so far unscathed, was girding up his loins for an encounter with a holiday crowd of about 200-300 (who were beginning to get restive because they had seen some bananas - then virtually unobtainable, and only there on that afternoon, because one of the committee members owned a banana importers' at Portsmouth). Oh yes, they wanted the bananas; for us, the bananas were the bait to make them listen to our speaker - if they could buy the bananas now, they would be off like a shot.

Our speaker, however, at this stage had the misfortune to catch his trouser leg on a strand of the barbed wire that had been hidden by the overgrown grass, ripping the coupon-precious Savile Row suit so that it flapped disconsolately around his leg. "I'm so sorry," I said. "That's all right," he said, bravely. Meanwhile, our lady chairman was telling everyone what an angel I had been in coming that afternoon.

We clambered on to the farm cart; by this time the crowd was getting really impatient - it was a holiday crowd, from strange far-off places and did not consist of our usual gentlemanly Pagham people. They were (or some of them were) shouting such rough remarks as "Get a move on;" and "We want to get back to the beach."

The limping Mrs. Farey-Jones was helped on to the farm cart - protesting that she was all right, thank you; it was quite all right, really. And in the background, the voice of the ever grateful lady chairman saying to all within earshot what an angel Barry had been in coming along. Our speaker by now was on the farm-cart, looking rather self-conscious I thought, about his trouser leg which flapped about in the high wind - gentlemen do not bare their legs when engaged upon such a high purpose, or they didn't in those days, anyway.

I began to speak by welcoming Mr. Farey-Jones for having come down from London especially to address us; all would have been well, had I left it at that, but instead, I went on to extol the work Mr. Fairy-Jones had done and was doing, for the Party. Mr. Fairy-Jones - I hesitated. *Fairy*-Jones? My thought processes started to work overtime. *Fairy*-Jones? Odd sort of name; it couldn't be. Perhaps I had got it wrong - perhaps it was *Angel*-Jones? That was it, so I continued, "Mr. Angel-Jones has done ..." No, that didn't sound right either. So in the end I referred to him as just plain Mr. Jones, but I suppose I need not have worried really, for the speaker's words (and my own) would have been lost to the prevailing south-west wind and nobody would have heard anything anyway.

It was left for me to reflect on how tough was the course of the aspirant for parliamentary honours.

* * * * *

Years passed, and I was chairing a meeting of the Association of Councillors in the House of Commons. Our speaker was a delightful chap - a Labour M.P. called Arthur Blenkinsop - but the Secretary had omitted to give me an agenda.

However, I was so familiar with the early part of the meeting that I began without an agenda, and then, on the item of the speaker, I began to introduce him. He was so well-known; he had done so much etc. etc. and my introduction droned on and on. I was getting desperate. Ultimately, I had to say, "Excuse me, but what *is* your name?"

* * * * *

My very first assistant at the *J.P.* was a former headmaster, one Alfred Tustin, known to me as Augustus on account of his years and former occupation. He had retired before the outbreak of War; came back for a couple of years, and then went to Butterworths for a job in their office. He must have been over 70 when he joined me in 1945; he was a delightful fellow, and of course, over the years, I got to know him and his history very well. He had been brought up as an orphan from the age of about six by an aunt who was matron, or master's wife, in a workhouse operating under the old Poor Law. He recounted that he remembered as a young boy hearing a nurse say to an old and sick man in the infirmary, "Die, won't you ... die, die, die." He left me to become a general handyman of some sort and his wife as cook-housekeeper, to be near their only son. Of course, it did not work out, and in due course they both ended their days in an old people's home; the authorities would not allow the wife, who was by this time well into her nineties, to sleep with him - so they both had to live out their lives in this enormous converted Poor Law institution never allowed (in effect) to even see each other. Life's full cycle ...

I used to send him a copy of the *J.P.* each week as I thought it might help to keep his mind active, and I knew he was fond of particular contributors - then one day I received an agonised letter from him begging me not to send him any further copies. It was part of the ethos of the firm to address every male subscriber as "Esquire" because apart from using it as a social courtesy, virtually all were either barristers or solicitors and therefore entitled to it as of right - apparently, the steward or male nurse or whatever his title was, who each morning distributed the post, would say, "Mr. John Smith, Mr. Bill Jones, Alfie Robinson - ah, and what have we here. We've actually got an Esquire" and he would go on to taunt poor dear Tustin unmercifully.

The humanity or lack of it, of parts of the Social Services sometimes left me astonished and this attitude has hardly improved with the passing years according to my observation.

In the days when the Association of Councillors held annual formal dinners, at one such my neighbour was Sir Harry Nicholas, the then General Secretary of the Labour Party and thus naturally one of the guests of honour. We were talking newspapers, and he said, "It may surprise you to know that as I have to travel so much all over the country, I find myself in a variety of hotel bedrooms with meetings to attend later in the morning, and that my choice of reading is *The Financial Times*. Why? I know I can get in a few moments all the hard factual news I need."

* * * * *

I hope not to be accused of *lèse-majestè* when I say that once, in the early 50s, I went to Arundel Castle for a garden party - and, with only Buckingham Palace as a bench-mark, I must say that the party at Arundel was, I fear I must say with enormous cheek, far superior. Two regimental bands played alternatively throughout the afternoon, and each of us queued to have our hands shaken by our host. In my case, I waited for what seemed an age, and then at last, shuffled forward to shake the ducal hand. Alas, when it came to my turn, the chap in front of me seemed to occupy a lot of our host's time. Then, he moved forward, and I stepped into the breach - but alas, as my hand stabbed empty space, so the Duke cried out, "Arthur, there's one more thing ..." and I gave way to A.E.R. Gillingham, the former England player and Sussex Captain.

I suspect the Duke's treasurer (or whatever he was called) would have expressed a view relating to this. Certainly of extragavance (tax then was, for someone like the Duke at a very high level, over 100 per cent), for I never heard of another garden party being given by him. I must say I admired him enormously, although I confess there were things about him I could not understand - for example, he had been my predecessor about 15 years previously as chairman of the Divisional Conservative Party - yet he disapproved of politics in local affairs; country pursuits were his life, and of course national affairs also. Gerry Reynolds (*q.v.*) when he was (Labour) Minister of War, told me he regarded Bernard Norfolk with tremendous admiration; for the interest he took, *inter alia*, in the Territorial Army; apparently the two 'hit it off'. As it happened, one morning I was on my way to see Gerry (who was in the last stages of terminal cancer) and as the train was about to enter Victoria Station, with the Duke in the next compartment, I wondered whether to tell him. However, there was no hint of recognition of me on his face, so I said nothing. I suppose if one is thrust into a public position by birth, there is always the threat of being bored out of one's mind by complete strangers or even by those who claim friendship. In retrospect, I think he was basically a very shy man to whom public duty was everything - I recall with pleasure one occasion when he seconded at county council a motion moved by me on the subject of fluoridation, with grace and elegance. We won; not that it did any good; 'they' have introduced it anyway.

One of my favourite stories about the Duke of Norfolk was told me by Dr. Geoghegan, medical officer of health for Arundel borough council (and also for Chichester R.D.C.). As a result of the crowds pouring into the town to visit the Castle, the town council decided that a public convenience should be made available in a certain spot on the Castle grounds. The Duke disagreed. The council said they insisted, and if the Duke persisted in his objection, they would get a compulsory purchase order. Apparently, the Duke (through his Agent) replied, "Very well. In that case I'll cut off your water supply."

When I first became chairman of the Chichester Conservative Constituency Association, there was in existence the Professional and Business Men's Luncheon Club - I remember presiding over the (9th) Duke of Richmond. He was a delightful man - he inherited thanks to death duties, an impoverished estate, which sedulously he sought to rebuild. Wisely, in my view, his son (as I write, the current Duke) was indentured as a chartered accountant and I have no doubt that the present finances of the ducal estate are once more on top line.

On this particular occasion, we chatted in the friendliest fashion possible, but the clock was ticking and came the time to use the gavel. As I rose, I had to address him by his title, and our easy relationship had to be put back on hold. Such formal phraseology as "His Grace" had to enter the scene; just down the road was the other Duke - Norfolk - to whom informality was wholly inappropriate. So, after a few warm-up lines such as to how privileged we were to have with us - someone we all knew and liked enormously - His Grace the Duke of *Norfolk*. The meeting was convulsed. When the noise moderated, I made my cover-up by explaining the difference between the two Dukes, and as he rose to speak, he said out of the corner of his mouth that I had got out of that one rather well.

It must have been 20 years later, in Chichester, when someone who had been a member of that luncheon club, and whom I had not seen in the interim, stopped me in the street and after a few words of greeting, asked whether I had said what I had said *on purpose*. He had often wondered. Twenty years on! He had worried about it for 20 years! Some you cannot win.

* * * * *

I have mentioned local government on a number of occasions - I must plead for the anonymity of the person concerned in the following, bearing in mind what was said. We hear a lot of the North/South Divide, and in local government there is a similar divide between elected members and appointed officers.

As a result of my ambivalent position in local government - editing a professional journal for officers on the one hand, and being an elected councillor on the other, sometimes led to things being said which perhaps would have been better left unsaid or at least unheard - for example, one treasurer of my acquaintance said that at each monthly council meeting, he was ashamed to be in the same chamber as his members. One can see what he meant: his professionalism as opposed to their amateurism. It is not of course only in local government that there is this feeling: I am currently publishing an autobiography written by (probably) the country's leading penologist; earlier in his career he was Private Secretary to the Earl of Home, before he became Prime Minister, and he recounts how he alerted Home to a clause in a Bill with which he was quite certain Lord Home would have disagreed. Because of its technicality, and almost certainly because of the way it was hidden away in the Bill, Home would not have spotted it or its significance.

Home thereafter was very much on his guard with the officials, and relied upon his Private Office - I mention this to illustrate that amateur v. professional is as old and as obvious as the North/South divide and is to be found in almost every level of our society.

* * * * *

My friend was an OE, "The Slough Tech", and we were discussing the activities of another, also an Old Etonian. "I don't know why it is, Barry, but Eton seems to produce two entirely different kinds of people - those who are all right, and those who are absolute s--- s." We both agreed that this particular person was in the category of a super s--t.

Another OE told me that (pre-war) while at Eton, he formed a branch of the Communist Party: the only problem was that it was a branch consisting only of himself - he could persuade no one else to join.

* * * * *

I mention Robert Maxwell because we were next to each other at a semi-private business dinner at the Dorchester. The host was Peter Fleck, my then vice-chairman at Chichester Constituency Conservative Association - a man of outstanding capabilities whose early death following a minor road accident robbed England of someone who would have developed into a major player in industry (and possibly also, in politics). He put me next to Maxwell, as he thought two publishers would find plenty to talk about.

From about 1947 onwards, I had heard of he who is now universally regarded as the villainous Robert Maxwell; F.W.S. Emery, then my managing director, kept me posted as from that date roughly as to what was going on in relation to Butterworths - I was in Chichester, some 60 miles away from where the real action was, and as a consequence I imagine he thought that what he said to me would remain confidential: so, largely, it has, until now. He said to me on one occasion, "God knows what Maxwell has cost Butterworths" and he estimated it at over £400,000 which in the late 1940s was a substantial sum ... some of us would think it is even today.

Emery was a chartered accountant, not a publisher, so he was not in any way to blame, and saw his role, at that time particularly, as a drag-chain to slow down what he regarded as somewhat reckless adventures, one of which Maxwell was to propose. Apparently Maxwell had come to Butterworths - remember, he was a Czech who had been commissioned in the field during the War by Montgomery, and therefore was presumed to know what he was about in the then devastated and murky world of European publishing and said to their directors - hardly one of them a publisher, but city solicitors, financiers, insurance brokers, etc., that as a result of the War, the great German scientific publishing house of Axel Springer was flat on the floor - bombed out of existence. In terms of scientific publishing, it had been the largest in the world, and the way was all clear for Butterworths to step in and fill the void.

Given that Butterworths were law and medical publishers and were delicately - ever so delicately - dipping their corporate toe into the cold and deep waters of tax and accountancy publishing, it was hardly (I would have thought) a very sensible thing to do at that particular time, but naturally, I was guided in my thoughts by what Emery said - and at that time, the real power in Butterworths seemed to vest in a man called Hugh Quennell.

He was everything that Emery was not: Emery (not a racing man) told me they had spent an afternoon at Goodwood, and Quennell had backed Gordon Richards, then champion jockey, £500.00 each race; at the end of the afternoon, he was £3,200 in pocket, and put the whole lot on Richards' mount in the last race, which, of course, lost. Emery was traumatised by this; from his point of view, he could see Maxwell and Quennell between them ruining the firm, and I hope that the main beneficiaries of Stanley Shaw Bond's Estate have remembered Emery thankfully in their prayers each night, in taking the firm through very perilous waters at that time.

Quennell was a solicitor (a former partner of Slaughter & May, one of the "magic circle" of city law firms), not a publisher, and was also a director of a number of other companies, including the British and Dominion Film Corporation. Presumably he had heard of Alfred Hitchcock appearing in a minor role of every film he directed, and he (Quennell) decided that this was the sort of path towards immortality he too should tread, for he issued the edict that each film was to mention his name somewhere in the script. Thus, *Springtime in Park Lane*, a light romantic comedy, had dear Anna Neagle in the middle of one scene, answering a telephone, and saying, "Hello, Mr. Quennell. Yes, Mr. Quennell" or having some equally pointless dialogue, before replacing the receiver. This indeed brought glamour by a short remove to the Butterworths' board, but it was to be short-lived.

One day, Emery told me that Quennell had resigned from the board of the British and Dominion Film Corporation because he was tired of the temperamental behaviour of the actors and actresses. Those of us who were Quennell watchers, however, saw an interesting shareholders' meeting reported in the *Daily Express* some three months after his resignation from the board of the said corporation, where one shareholder - showing proper dismay at the enormous losses for the previous 12 months, inquired why no profit warning had been made and why an interim dividend had been declared when manifestly the company had been operating at a loss at the time, and said he thought Mr. Quennell's activities should be investigated by the Director of Public Prosecutions.

It was not very long afterwards that the *Evening Standard* was to report that Mr. Quennell had resigned from Butterworths' board and was on a "slow boat to China" (the actual phrase used, presumably borrowed from the name of a song popular at that time). I did hear the reason for his departure from Butterworths which I fear was not to his credit, but I am more concerned here to explain how Maxwell received the support of Quennell - a man incidentally I never met and who had never been a member of the

J.P. board, but whose influence seemed to pervade everywhere and everything in Butterworths - even to the extent (so it was said) of making Butterworths' (then) poor little *Law Journal* have a cover printed in his racing colours. Oh what it is to be a Press Lord - or rather, what it is to *think* one is a Press Lord.

I do not suppose for a moment that Maxwell would have got what he wanted had anyone but Quennell been in charge of negotiations which led to the relatively short-lived Butterworths-Springer company from whence sprang Maxwell's Pergamon. Of course, over the years I had heard various matters very much to Maxwell's discredit - such as a firm of book wholesalers - to the dismay of publishers everywhere - being forced into bankruptcy; a rather high profile silk (at the time of writing, now retired as a deputy High Court Judge) telling me that he had been on the periphery of that matter and could never understand why the DPP's Department had never prosecuted; of Robert Fleming, the merchant bankers, having been taken for a ride by Maxwell (twice!), and the Board of Trade Inquiry finding that he was not fit to be a director of any public company.

I knew all this and more when I sat next to him at dinner; he did not (unlike the rest of us) wear a black tie, but a white polo neck sweater, yet the extraordinary thing was - despite everything I had heard about him - I rather liked him. In the intervening years, he had made a bid for Butterworths so that Butterworths - to escape his unwelcome embrace - were forced into the arms of I.P.C. (the owners, then, of the *Daily Mirror*). He appeared very hurt that his overtures to buy Butterworths had been rejected, and that I.P.C. had won control, and said to me, "My bid increased Mrs. Bond's [long since Mrs. Willis] holding by £4m. and she does not even send me a postcard of thanks."

* * * * *

Come to think of it, Mrs. Bond was always rather sparing in her thanks to the men and women who had made her life fairly comfortable - she had married Bond when she was very young and when he was rather old: he was also very rich. He was Treasurer of the Church of England, and either chairman or president of the Bachelors' Club, a position he presumably had to relinquish on his marriage, and she I was told had known (despite being the granddaughter of an earl) some privation in early life. I remember her particularly when I appeared at a dinner of my last staff association meeting for Butterworths; I then had to propose something or other (the nature of which I now forget). Instead of starting with a graceful thank-you to the lady member of staff who had presented her with flowers, and perhaps a word for me, she launched straight into a speech (on a social occasion, mark you) which amounted to an harangue saying that she was dissatisfied with the profitability of the company and she and her advisers were to make changes of which we, the workforce, might disapprove, but they were going ahead anyway.

Of course, one would not have expected anyone of her background to have appreciated that the workforce could only perform as directed by those like dear lamented Mr. Quennell, whom she and the trust brought into existence presumably under the terms of her late husband's will as a result of Death Duties - to paraphrase Lloyd-George, "it is not only soldiers who can be lions led by donkeys - it can apply to companies, too." For myself, I never again went to any function likely to be attended by Mrs. Willis. Not of course for a single instant have I thought my absence would have been noticed.

* * * * *

James Comyn became a dear friend, and some years later, godfather to my daughter, Diana - he was a very successful barrister; he once told me he thought he was probably the first member of the Bar to top £100,000 in annual earnings. He wrote short, snappy pieces of verse which I used in the *J.P.* - alas, I fear it added but little to his income, but they amused our readers and I was glad to have them for filling the odd space at the bottom of the column in an otherwise very serious publication.

He took silk at 36 - said to be the youngest of his generation - but his life was marred by the "black dog" depressions which fortunately became lessened in frequency and severity after his marriage to Anne.

On his appointment to the Bench he was allocated to the Family Division, but soon asked to be transferred to the Queen's Bench Division, as he could not bear the unhappiness he had to witness in the former court, and seemed happier among the criminal lawyers and with the common law generally.

Probably the *cause célèbre* for which he will be best remembered in the public mind is the *Alfie Hinds* case. Hinds had been convicted of the Maples Store robbery and received a long term of imprisonment as a consequence. He maintained that although he had had a string of convictions in his early life, after his marriage to Rose (to avoid possibly confusion, this reference is to his wife, not to the Author!), he had led a blameless existence, and had been nowhere near Maples when the robbery took place. In other words, he claimed he was stitched up.

To establish his innocence, he escaped from prison on a number of occasions, always offering to return voluntarily if he would be granted a new trial. Well, those of us "in the trade" had heard all that sort of thing before, yet after a particularly imaginative escape (at the Royal Courts of Justice, no less) John Edye - my deputy at that time - and myself were discussing it one morning - and both of us, after admiring the skill and audacity of Mr. Hinds, had the thought simultaneously that perhaps, just *perhaps*, he was indeed innocent.

John spent about five days (by my recollection) away from the office for research; he came back convinced as to Hinds' innocence, and wrote a longish article on the subject. Well, the article hardly painted the police in a very favourable light, and in effect was a "campaigning" article. I got it cleared by Goodman Derrick, our libel lawyers, and also by the chief legal editor of Butterworths, our owners. It was still, manifestly, a campaigning article; however, had I then owned the *J.P.* I would have published it forthwith - but the *J.P.* was not and had never been a campaigning journal, and I thought it advisable - since it went beyond the parameters I had followed - to get clearance for it from the managing director. He thought it a good article, but foresaw trouble with the Police Service (then comprising a substantial proportion of our readership) and the Home Office if published in the *J.P.* but said he did not mind it appearing anywhere else and suggested the *Spectator*.

The *Spectator* said it was an excellent article, and they would like to publish but that it was too long - would John care to cut and re-submit? By this time, John was bored by the whole subject - but then Detective Superintendent Sparks wrote his autobiography, and was foolish enough to mention the villain Hinds and the Maple Robbery - which gave Mr. Hinds his chance - from his prison cell, he sued for libel, and James Comyn acted for him. Disgrace for Sparks, victory for Hinds, and he was released from prison immediately. The Establishment, however, was not going to be caught a second time, so Parliament was asked to outlaw the bringing of libel cases from a prison cell. Comyn would always speak as if he had a soft spot for Alfie Hinds. These days, I suppose

Hinds would have received an enormous sum in compensation for deprivation of liberty, but then, so far as I know, he received nothing.

* * * * *

While he was still at the Bar, I got a call from James suggesting a meal in Chichester, as he was involved in a case there at quarter sessions and had to stay overnight. Over dinner he mentioned the nature of the case: it concerned a veterinary surgeon on a manslaughter charge. Apparently the accused had pulled from his trouser pocket an humane killer and used it to its designed effect upon a man who (to use that old-fashioned expression) had trifled with his wife's affections. He (Comyn) had advised that the defendant when giving evidence, to refer to "Exhibit 'A'" and never to mention the words "humane killer" because the unfortunate effect he thought this might have on the jury. However, the accused had done just that: as a result, James was gloomy in his prognostications as to the outcome. A tribute indeed to his oratorical skill came the next day, when the man was found not guilty.

* * * * *

Years passed, and I met the son of a friend who had moved from Worthing to Pulborough, then a village, now a small town, in West Sussex. It so happened he was with the Crown Prosecution Service, whose predecessors would have had some part to play in the case just mentioned. But that is by the way.

I have little doubt that after the move to the new house, both he and his wife were exhausted. It is easy to visualise the scene when, about 1 o'clock in the morning, his wife nudged him awake, asking, "What was that?" "What was what?" "There was a noise." "I daresay, but I'm tired; go back to sleep." Silence and peace. Then another nudge, "What is it?" "How should I know?" and then *he* heard it. "Sounds like a lion" he would have volunteered. "Don't be silly - this is Pulborough, not Regent's Park. Of course it's not a lion." But in the cold light of morning, that's just what it was - in the garden of the house next door, owned by the same veterinary surgeon who had figured in the Comyn case years before at Chichester - I suppose the lion was to ward off any future unwelcome suitors for his wife's affections.

James Comyn introduced me to Leslie Starke, who illustrated Comyn's books, one of which was of humorous verse, which he called *Poetic Justice*, and which he dedicated "To the man on the Clapham omnibus, who has to stand so much" one of the wittier dedications I can remember.

Leslie Starke was a cartoonist much admired in his time. He was I believe the first cartoonist to hold an exhibition (a retrospective, in pompous language) of his work. Initially, in the late 1940s, he illustrated jackets of books I published for the *J.P.* (and also would illustrate chapters in the books themselves). Later, a cartoon by him would adorn each issue of the monthly *Police Journal*, which I then owned - his capacity to find humour in any subject was something I found quite remarkable. Even before the War, he was well-known - his work would appear in *Punch* when it *was Punch* and a whole range - an astonishingly wide range - of other journals and newspapers. Although we had a long association, I met him only once, when he lunched with me.

He told me that in 1938, he was invited to go to the United

States as cartoonist for the *New Yorker*; he thought it over, and in the end decided against on the grounds that he knew what made England tick, and was a bit too old to start again in a different country. "But," he said, "d'you know - throughout the War, they always sent me food parcels. Wasn't that nice of them?" I imagine it would have been the legendary Ross who would have arranged that; I am glad Starke did not go, as he was able to add much to the comic scene in this country, then much in need of it.

I give one of his cartoons here - it was intended for a local government journal which never took off so this is the first time it has appeared anywhere.

* * * * *

The T.U.C., through one of its affiliated unions, the National Union of Journalists, oddly enough was responsible for bringing John Edye and myself together. John and his wife Alison lived on a houseboat on the Thames - he worked at Foyles, the bookshop in Charing Cross Road, until one day he returned to his houseboat and discovered it was sinking. He and his wife, wishing to avoid the expense of clearing the boat from where he feared it would presently lie (at the bottom of the river and therefore a threat to navigation) saved as many of the contents as it was possible to save, and ultimately came to live in Chichester where he opened a bookshop. The houseboat - he fervently hoped - would not, with the expense of its removal, be tracked down to him.

The family moved to a rather beautiful pair of cottages in Sidlesham, close to Pagham Harbour, and shortly afterwards John became blind. Ultimately, this was established to have been caused by an allergy to goats' hair - which had been used in the making of plaster a century or so before in the said cottages, and which had caused his blindness; in the meantime he had to dispose of his shop and look around for something to do. He thought journalism might provide the answer, but in that public spirited way in which British journalism operated at that time and probably still does, it was on the closed shop principle, where the National Union of Journalists was king. Because, very naturally, journalists at that time were broadly protected by the N.U.J. and had negotiated a local agreement - a sort of 9 a.m. - 5 p.m. arrangement, resulting in there being no one, generally, to cover the later more minor stories; they were generous enough to allow John to work as a freelance, even although he did not have N.U.J. membership, provided this was outside their hours. Thus it was that John came to regard me - as he put it - as his weekend leg of lamb, since invariably (so it seemed) I was always at evening meetings which he was to report and was subsequently to be paid.

Ultimately, I suggested he should join me at the *J.P.*; he was a truly extraordinary man. His wife was an officer in the W.R.N.S., so his courtship of her as a Royal Marine would not have been without its difficulties - although with a background which included Harrow School and Balliol, a "natural" in those days for commissioned rank, he declined, preferring to remain in the ranks. He was a journalist of rare ability (see for example p.38 relating to Alfie Hinds) and after he joined me it represented a tremendous easing of my own burden - when at one time we were taken over by I.P.C. (a hard-line closed shop headed by the N.U.J.) there were three of us in the *J.P.* who were members of the Institute of Journalists - a very gentlemanly union which in its constitution specifically excluded the right of its members to strike; the N.U.J. got in touch with me and at their request, I arranged a luncheon with their organiser, for the three of us; I took them to a favourite and rather expensive restaurant at the Union's expense; we listened to the picture that was painted for us. I think all three of us, as we listened, knew that the journal would not be able to afford such terms and would be doomed and all three of us rejected the offer to join the N.U.J.

And as for the Houseboat? The last time John saw it was, figuratively, sinking below the waves at the Thames anchorage. And now? John was walking with his family, along Birdham Canal, and what should they see? Their houseboat. How it got there, he evidently deemed it not worth pursuing.

* * * * *

Most of the men I knew who had fought in the First World War never spoke about their (for the most part) horrific experiences, and I recall reading David Lloyd-George's account of that War before the Second World War (and I've read it again since, as I have read other works by War historians, etc.). The image of appalling generalship still remains a bad memory and I made a very definite oath that if I were ever fortunate enough (or the nation unfortunate enough) for me to become an M.P., I would, apart from supporting my Party on major issues, dedicate myself to trying to effect the removal of Haig's statue from Whitehall which I regard as an insult almost, to the lives of those who were killed as a result of his generalship. Nothing I have read or heard, nothing I have seen on reconstituted newsreels etc., has persuaded me to a contrary opinion over the past 60 years - a dreadful general, and a dreadful man. I remember with some clarity some of the former soldiers saying to me, "Well, of course no one could tell the public the truth, for if they had there would have been a near revolution." Well, I don't know about that, but I do know my opinion has if anything hardened over the years by remarks made by chaps like Noel Williamson (*q.v.*), who was an officer in the Artillery (and subsequently when I knew him, the senior surviving officer of the British Expeditionary Force to Russia at the end of the First War).

He told me that, at the Somme, after the massive bombardment when our guns had pounded the German lines for weeks on end, he sat back when it ceased and watched through his glasses our chaps struggling over the top of the trenches wearing their full kit (I think it weighed 84 lbs.) and then lying down in the sun, sun-bathing. His first thought that this was not the idea at all - they should be advancing and taking over the German trenches. Instead of that, the poor men were dead or seriously wounded; the Germans had come out of their re-inforced trenches when the bombardment ceased, and just massacred our men as they advanced. Of course, it had never occurred to the General Staff and Haig as their Commander who had to take full responsibility, that the Germans might reinforce their trenches. Never mind, Haig had still plenty of reserves to fall back upon ... And to be fair, Noel took Haig's part in the arguments we had about the Somme, and I have to say, *he* was actually there.

Another friend, a Q.C. called Bill Williams, whenever I met him, never failed to drink a toast to Fritz, the anonymous German who had shot him at the Battle of Messines, so that he was wounded and thus missed the slaughter of the Somme.

Bill Williams had a remarkable career: after the first World War, he qualified as a solicitor and became Deputy Clerk of the Peace for Middlesex. When the Clerk of the Peace retired, the council in its wisdom did not appoint Bill as his successor.

Bill, I think a little hurt, left Middlesex and switched to the Bar; became a Doctor of Laws and, later, a Silk. He also became editor of various editions of *Ryde on Rating*, the classic work on Rating Law. He claimed for himself an unusual record - his clerk had double-booked him, that is to say, he was booked to appear at Maidstone and at Southend-on-Sea in separate cases at the same time. He completed his case at Maidstone, and then hired a plane to fly him to Southend to appear in his case there - the first barrister ever to have surmounted that well-known difficulty in this way.

I fear as a result of his friendship with me, he left Surrey and came down to live in Bognor - but alas, he did not take into account the high winds which are that resort's speciality in the autumn, and, battling against them to get into an hotel for a drink, while his wife took the cab on for her shopping, had a heart attack. I was at a meeting or in London (I forget which) and Jean was called by his widow Jane to their home. Dear Bill had died; it was the first time that Jean had seen a dead body; and because the gales had claimed others that day, the undertakers were some time in coming. He had died whilst reading a legal biography, and the book had just slipped between his legs. A very nice way to go, but decidedly upsetting for his widow. During the Second World War, he and his wife had a suite on top of the Savoy, on the theory that if they were to be killed, it was better that way than to be buried alive.

He once met me for luncheon at Simpson's - and in the vestibule he asked how was Diana. Diana had been born two days earlier, and an announcement had duly appeared in *The Times*, &c. that morning - parenthood was a new experience for me - but his question had me absolutely stumped. Diana. Who was Diana?

Bill was an authority on Rating and Valuation Law, and also Town and Country Planning. His reputation continued for many years after his death - everyone seemed to admire his intellect, and, unusually in my experience, always referred to him as "Doctor" Williams, even chaps like Sir Desmond Heap, who was the City's guru on planning and the originator of Heap's *Encyclopaedia of Planning Law*, and Frank Othick, the "expert" on rating law.

Middlesex had turned him down - but then, I have yet to meet the solicitor who switched to the other side of the profession and regretted the move.

* * * * *

I tell what follows affecting the "domestic" side of office life in view of its conclusion, which has little meaning without a knowledge of what went before.

When Butterworths acquired the *J.P.* from Mrs. Myrtle Bond, who had been left it by her husband, Stanley Shaw Bond, who had begun his astonishingly successful publishing career on the *J.P.* before he became the owner of Butterworths. Very naturally, Bond had a great affection for the journal, and when in England up to the outbreak of War, I am told, he always made a practice of opening its post himself; he said it was Butterworths in miniature. When Mrs. Bond sold it to Butterworths it made very little difference -

most of the directors of Butterworths were also directors of the *J.P.* and as before, Emery was the managing director of the *J.P.* but very naturally, Butterworths wished for the harmonisation of the accounts, and an individual from their accounts department was dispatched to Chichester for this purpose. Our own accounts were in meticulous order - our auditors/accountants had seen to that - the objective therefore was to tie in our system with that of Butterworths, which to me seemed reasonable enough. The chap they sent down to effect this seemed, however (to my Chichester eyes) quite extraordinary - the impression soon became inescapable that he had an unhappy home life, and spending his time in Chichester, staying at the then best (at any rate, most expensive) hotel, seemed very much to his liking.

However, what should (in my opinion) have been an exercise lasting perhaps one or two weeks extended into a period of months. Technically speaking, as I didn't own the company and wasn't paying for this chap's time or his hotel bills, it was nothing to do with me, but I was aware of tension in my office. The tension burst when my secretary came to see me, speaking on behalf of all the lady members of the staff, to complain about what would today be called sexist remarks from this individual, such as discussing the size of their breasts and other matters of a highly personal nature. (Today, I suppose even with the coarsening of our society since those days, the firm would have been taken to the Employment Tribunal straight away: then, it was quite horrific with no statutory remedy for the young ladies concerned.) Earlier, he had made clear to me that he was determined to see that one poor girl would be sacked (this long before any statutory provision against wrongful dismissal had been enacted) but I had no idea that his behaviour with other women in the office was a cause for complaint. (So far as the unfortunate girl was concerned - I had found her work quite satisfactory and warned her what was in the wind; indeed I helped her compose a job application which was successful; it may be of interest to remark in passing that she subsequently founded her own business in the West End of London, and apparently was eminently successful.)

But what was I to do with this far more serious matter? Unfortunately, Emery (my managing director who was also a director of Butterworths) was on a tour of Canada - so I could not get in touch with him; instead, I informed the individual's own head of department, and asked for the man to be removed from my office. I would have thought that any person of the meanest intelligence would have known that there could not be a rational reason why the harmonisation of our tiny set of accounts should have taken so long. Instead, he informed me he had informed the individual of my formal complaint, and kept him in my offices until Emery's return a month or so later, who of course, instantly removed him. It takes very little to imagine the atmosphere in my office during this period.

Down the road from the *J.P.* was another company recently acquired by Butterworths - very much larger than the *J.P.*, and which did a lot of work for it. As by then I had been in a relatively senior position in the firm for some six or seven years I was asked to be friendly to the new manager they had acquired to run this firm; naturally we met for luncheon at about monthly intervals. Very naturally again, at one of those luncheons, I would have mentioned the worry caused by this chap from Butterworths in the ordinary course of conversation. He seemed friendly enough, and on one occasion introduced me to his fiancée - a girl in the Foreign Office who, according to him, had been smuggled out of Yugoslavia at the time of Tito in a packing case. Or into. Anyway, I remember a packing case was involved.

On another occasion he told me with a laugh he was in a bit of trouble, as a girlfriend he had had in New York was coming over to see him; she was, he told me, a member of one of the leading families in the United States - this would cause problems with his fiancée, as the New York girl was proposing to stay with him. In due course, he introduced me to her: even now, I blush at the recollection and why I should have believed him. She was plainly a nice working girl, and I would imagine was not even the most distant cousin of the famous family of which she was said to be a member. I addressed her formally by the name he had previously given me, and she looked at him sharply as if to say, "What's he been telling this guy?" Well, it was nothing to do with me, and in due course I retreated to my office, mildly curious to know why this perfectly nice and respectable girl had been made a connection with one of the most dreadful but also one of the richest of the infamous "robber barons" in America.

Weeks passed, and then I was informed that Emery was giving me a visit in the afternoon - the first time since he had returned from Canada, and he was to see the manager of the other Butterworth company in the morning. He mentioned the matter of the accounts and said he removed the individual the cause of the trouble and had appointed someone else to keep an eye on our accounts on a quarterly basis to see they were kept in line with Butterworths requirements and that was that. We did not discuss the individual concerned and his main conversation was to tell me about his trip to Canada.

Peace reigned, weeks passed, and then I was having my quiet luncheon in Chichester in the *Unicorn* - a farmers' pub now alas closed - when I was aware that two pretty girls were smiling at me across the room. I was mildly curious as to who they were, but left the restaurant to return to my office without making contact.

My grandly named reception office then told me that a Miss X had called to see me; the name meant nothing to me but I said I would see her - it was one of the two girls I had seen in the restaurant. Because so many months had passed I did not recognise her; I had been introduced to her as the fiancée of the colleague at the printing factory down the road. She knew about the New York girlfriend, and she desperately wanted help from me: did I know whether this girl really meant anything to her fiancé or not? He had a cruel streak in him, she said - he knew what terrible trouble I was in as having stolen the petty cash from my firm ... Of course, at this stage, I leapt out of my chair, almost hitting the ceiling, and said all the usual things. That being the case, I was determined to do what I could to help her - she was with me from about 2.15 until past 7 p.m. - everything she told me about him I was able to rebut as a result of various reference books I had in my office - for example, she said his father was a barrister; I referred to the *Law List* which at that time was virtually the only directory in existence relating to the Bar and was able to prove that this individual's father was not a barrister ("Well, Barry, I thought it funny, because he wore carpet slippers when we called at their house") and there were about half a dozen other matters which I was able to satisfy her that he had lied to her. At the end, she asked me what to do, "You have a flat in London; catch the next train to London and forget this chap ever existed."

This she said she would do. The next morning, at about 9.30, she telephoned and said, "Barry, you're in deadly danger. Last night after I left you I decided to have a confrontation with him, and he said, 'You've been talking to Barry Rose. I'll kill him,' and Barry, he will. He's got a revolver, I've seen it in his desk - he's going to kill you."

Well, the building has been pulled down now, but anyone who

remembers my office of those days would remember that my interior walls were made of a sort of *papier mâché* material, and the doors would succumb to the slightest pressure from outside. All I had to defend myself with was a 19th century heavy ebony ruler; I kept the doors locked from the inside, and held on to that ruler every time I heard someone walk down the corridor outside. Scared? You must be kidding. I was petrified.

I demanded to see Emery; he could not fit me in except on the Saturday morning - he seemed very cool, calm and collected. "A jealous woman," he said, and told me not to worry.

Later that month, I met the individual concerned for our usual luncheon. "What would you like to drink, Barry?" and nothing else was said. A short time later, he was to leave the firm, and he asked me to write a letter giving him a reference - I did so - a letter composed with great care.

* * * * *

Mr. Ron Stone, Q.P.M., once invited me to the annual dinner of the Chief Constables' Club, which met at the London Guildhall. A most impressive gathering, and I found myself next to someone from the Home Office who discussed with me the then recent Poll Tax Riots. He told me that had the Commissioner not correctly assessed the situation likely to develop, and had put into the field 500 less police, Downing Street itself could have been sacked. I confess that until then, I had not realized just how desperately important it is for the Police to correctly interpret the signs and portents of likely demonstrations - most demonstrators, of course, were merely vocally making their objections heard and violence was the last thing in their thoughts - but the hard core was using them, and on the Monday following the Saturday riots, I was in a cab in St

Martin's Lane entering upon Trafalgar Square. The cabbie told me he had been out in the thick of it, and had been on his way to take a party to the R.A.C. Club in Pall Mall. He quickly altered his route, as he had been genuinely fearful not only for his passengers who were in evening dress and therefore a prime target for unruly minds, but also for his cab - he saw one huge fellow smash a plate glass window with a baseball bat.

* * * * *

My neighbour at the Chief Constables' Club dinner was, as I have said, from the Home Office. The General Election of 1980 was then only about 12 months behind us, where I had stood as an Alternative Conservative against Mr. Edward Heath (as he then was) and where I had been told in an official letter that I had overspent the permitted maximum expenditure by some £4,000 and was, in consequence, to be prosecuted. This arose as a result of my perpetual inefficiency (I had lost the letter informing me the maximum expenditure to be allowed, but in any event, mine was not a lavish campaign); nevertheless, I was hoping to make political capital out of the prosecution when it came by claiming that the candidates of all the major parties were in breach of the same law - for example, if either the Conservative Party or the Labour Party is in credit by say £5m. before an election, and is in debt to the tune of £20m. after it with the inference that £25m. has been actually spent on the election - if this money is divided on a proportional basis throughout the country, by say 630 constituencies, it will be seen that a considerable amount of money is being spent on newspaper and poster advertising, as well as all sorts of fees for publicity consultants and so on all in addition to the amounts returned by the candidates as their actual expenditure so that in truth, *all* were overspent. Alas, I was to be denied being prosecuted, and through counsel pleading along these lines - I asked my neighbour - why no prosecution? He said that there were a lot of candidates at the election who would be coming up for prosecution, and it took some time for them to work their way through. I have heard nothing more. Alas. But the Government has since undertaken to modernise the whole matter of electoral expenses (so perhaps my words got back! But I do not advance this seriously, although perhaps ... just perhaps ...).

Later, I will describe how I came to oppose Heath.

* * * * *

Sir George Mallaby I shall always remember for his love of vodka and tomato juice (Bloody Mary's) - I got to know him quite well when he was part of our team of lecturers for courses on local government - he had just produced his Report on Management in Local Government. He was, as I understand it, Second Secretary to the Cabinet, and he told me that there had not been a Cabinet member from Attlee onwards he had not known. He said to me once, that had he been invited to two dinner parties which clashed - one where Harold Wilson would be present, and one where Edward Heath, he would unhesitatingly choose that to be attended by Wilson. He was responsible for chairing the body to revise the Rules for Rugby Football. In this instance, he was invited to their beanfeast, where Heath had also been invited - Mallaby turned his face to the wall of the private reception area as he just did not wished to be spotted by Heath.

Curious this dislike for Heath. A friend of mine (alas now dead) was a sailmaker (Bob Bowker, of Bosham) and Bowker received an order from Ted Heath for his yacht 'Morning Cloud'.

Apparently some details had to be sorted out, so Bob sent his foreman to see him; the following morning he was curious to know what his foreman thought of the Great Man. Apparently, not very much.

* * * * *

In the post-War years, because of the relatively low salaries paid to M.P.s, it was more or less incumbent upon some of them, those without private incomes, to earn money in their parliamentary time. As there were fearsome numbers of barristers and solicitors in the House at that time (about 130 or thereabouts I seem to remember), it was natural that a percentage would gravitate to legal journalism. Thus, in the days when - by the standards of today - there was virtually no security, I found myself going to Parliament to meet various contributors. It seems in retrospect almost unbelievable but I would go to "Annie's Bar" with my Member contributor, buy ourselves a drink, and then have a chat thanking him for what he had done and discuss future contributions. "Security" was non-existent, and I had to go so frequently I was accepted as 'a member of the club'.

As parliamentary salaries climbed, obviously there was no longer the pressing need for Members to write for us, and my visits became fewer, until they petered out altogether. Years later, when Bill Loveys (*q.v.*) became our local M.P. and I was his chairman, I met him about 4 p.m. in the Lobby the same week he was elected and suggested a drink. As a "new boy" he did not know that the bars of the House were open all the time the House was sitting, and I took him to Annie's Bar - it had been so long since I had been there, that mine was no longer a fairly familiar face, and the barmaid said "Your name and constituency, Sir." So I was rumbled, and if I may say so, rightly so. But one of our contributors became a friend outside the House - Graeme Finlay.

He was such a delightful chap, with a lovely sense of humour, and fed me various titbits of gossip, one of which concerned Winston - the great Winston. Apparently, he would be in the Chamber and walk out as if the whole weight of the world was on his shoulders; one day, Graeme followed him and Winston almost literally galloped down the corridor when he thought no one was looking. Graeme, however, was booted out by boundary redistribution - three New Towns were built in Essex where he had his constituency - Epping, which almost completely altered the whole character of the county, and meant he lost his traditional Conservative Essex seat.

As still a fairly young barrister, he was out of a job, and because in a sense, whilst an M.P. and in a (junior) Government post and therefore unable to work at the Bar, he was virtually unknown as a barrister. He felt reluctant to starting again, and not disposed to travelling out to the suburbs of the Metropolis on some insignificant county court matter, and therefore sought a meeting with Lord Hailsham, then Lord Chancellor, to inquire if there was any possibility of getting a minor judicial appointment. Hailsham (whose pupil Finlay had been at the commencement of his career) was shocked, and said, "I can't do that - that would be nepotism."

Graeme ultimately ended up as Judge in Jersey, and perhaps more interestingly, as he previously had held a minor Government job, he received the last baronetage to be given to anyone until Sir Denis Thatcher, Bart., about 40 years later.

I recall he once told me he had been briefed to represent (in a libel action - therefore what promised to be an exceedingly high profile case) Dylan Thomas, who had been described in a newspaper article as a drunkard. Here was the case to make his fortune. Alas, before the case could come to court, Dylan died in an alcoholics' ward of a New York hospital - at least, that is how it was reported at the time, although later his death was ascribed to other causes. Poor Graeme, who told me it was the sort of case anyone would dream about. And poor Dylan too.

* * * * *

A lady member of our staff appeared one morning after having been to the Casualty Department of the local hospital. Her clothes were torn, she was badly bruised and her skin had been broken in one or two places. She had come into Chichester by moped. In Little London, Chichester, on the way to our offices is a taxi firm, which every morning washed its cars, the water draining away on the road outside. One bitterly cold morning, this water had frozen over, with the near disastrous but nevertheless quite damaging results I have mentioned. Naturally, I said this was a matter to be reported to the Police. An officer came, took a statement, and about a week later gravely informed her that they had decided to take no action against her.

* * * * *

Hugh (Lord) Cudlipp, for a short while, was my boss. This was when he was chairman of the mighty I.P.C., having deposed Lord King in a boardroom revolution. It was a period when Butterworths was an orphan in the storm, about to be swallowed up by the nasty and wicked Robert Maxwell (*q.v.*) and I.P.C. bought Butterworths out of pity to save it from such a fate. At least, that is one interpretation that can be put on it. Hugh had been editor of the *Daily Mirror* in its great days; he said to me once that he never joined the Labour Party until he retired - which was an indication of his journalistic integrity.

He was ennobled as Lord Cudlipp of Aldingbourne - coincidentally after the name of a parish in which he lived but which comprised part of the county council division I represented. He was great fun to be with, a wonderful supply of invective always on tap, a prodigious memory, and a biting wit. I was having a drink one Saturday with my wife in the *Ship* in Chichester, when Hugh came in. Somehow the subject turned to religion - a dangerous subject always - and Jean declared her faith, whereupon Hugh said, "And I'm a born-again atheist." Jean left the bar to go to the powder room and Hugh, with all the wicked innocence of a wilful child, "Did I say something to upset her?"

I remember a television debate between Peter Sheppard, then chairman of the West Sussex county council, some years after I had left it and Hugh, on that council's meanness towards the arts. Of course, Hugh (with his access to the huge library and news resources of the *Daily Mirror* which he still possessed although no longer editor) as well as his natural gifts, cut Peter to pieces; it was painful to watch. Hugh said to me afterwards, "Barry, I bet that if you were still Leader of the Group you would not have allowed him to have appeared with me." He was so right: the contest was pre-destined to be so one-sided.

The one occasion I have regretted not having been able to record a conversation by having a tape recorder under the table, which was when we had Sir Alfred Sherman and his wife and small son staying with us for the weekend, and we invited the Cudlipps over for dinner. The stimulation of two great minds clashing with one another from completely different political standpoints was a duel not to be forgotten: neither I nor Jean had ever witnessed or heard anything like it. It deserved to be recorded.

On the subject of recordings, I was invited by Harry Creighton (then the owner of the *Spectator* who died in July 2003) to his journal's private luncheons from time to time. On one occasion John Freeman, the former Ambassador to the US, was present; it was whilst the first suggestions were being made as to the possible impeachment of President Nixon, and I remember asking him whether, when he went to the White House, he himself had had the impression that he was being tape recorded. "Constantly," he replied. He had never been in the White House without experiencing such a sensation.

* * * * *

A Triumvirate of Editors - Reception at the Press Club, circa 1970s
Brian Harris, OBE, QC, Barry Rose, John S. Edye

I had a friend called Fred Adams. He was Royal Navy. He had joined the Navy as a boy before the turn of the 20th century, and had first gone to sea under sail. By the time I knew him, during the War, he was in charge of the anti-aircraft defences on Bognor Pier. (For those interested in such matters, it consisted of a Bofors Gun; I am not sure whether it had any ammunition - after all, there was a war on, and things were in short supply). He was in charge of young W.R.N.S. subordinate to him in his smart sub-lieutenant's uniform. He must have been at least 60 by this time - he certainly *looked* much older, but his wife Flo was jealous that one of these young W.R.N.S. would seduce him; therefore, she made a point of being with him always. She would hide in a clump of bushes at the bottom of Waterloo Square, as near to Bognor Pier as it was possible to get, and mounted watch. He told me with a chuckle that he pretended not to see her, and when offered a lift home by the W.R.N.S. on their way back to barracks or the naval equivalent, he left her behind in the bushes to find her own way.

It was not always thus. He told me after they had married, they went to Blackpool for their honeymoon, to a boarding house. They were shown into their bedroom, when the bride sniffed, and then sniffed again. "Fred," she said, "they've got mice here." The landlady was summoned. "There aren't any mice in this house," she declared with warmth. So, after she had left, "Fred," Flo said, "there *are* mice here. I know it." So Fred went out and bought a mousetrap. The next morning, they called the landlady in, and pointed to the mantelshelf where about half-a-dozen mice were laid in a row. "No mice, eh? What are these, then? Rabbits?"

Portsmouth FC was having a good season; Lord Montgomery was their President. Any Saturday Portsmouth was playing at home, Fred (naturally always accompanied by his wife) went to watch. However, by this time she had grown rather plump, and one

Saturday the turnstile jammed, with Mrs. Fred stuck in the middle of it. "Laugh," said this honest sailor, "I laughed until I cried."

The Navy can have a cruel side.

* * * * *

Another sailor I knew was Admiral "Jock" Hughes-Hallett - known to the Senior Service as "Hughes-Hitler" - presumably because of the strict discipline he enforced. On leaving the Navy on retirement, he became M.P. for one of the Croydon seats - and then Parliamentary Secretary to Ernest Marples when he was Minister of Transport: he told me they used to meet in Marples' flat once a week, for this was the only time they could speak and have a proper discussion without the presence of civil servants.

At Croydon, his constituency [before the creation of the G.L.C.] was politically in the County of Surrey, and therefore within the ambit of Jean when she was county chairman of Surrey Young Conservatives; they became quite good friends. This was before he retired from politics, and before Jean married me. He came to live in Slindon, which was part of Chichester constituency of which I was chairman; thus, he became the friend of both of us, especially when Peter Fleck (*q.v.*), who during the War had been captain's secretary to Hughes-Hallett, suggested Jock be president of the constituency association.

He was by far the most eccentric of all my friends. He once told me he had "sold" his body to be dissected after death - although I noticed, that after that death, he was cremated the same as everyone else, so I can only assume he had bought himself back again. He told me that once he had occasion to go to St Thomas's - just across the way from the Houses of Parliament and he was stripped under the orders of the specialist in front of a group of students. "Now tell me what this man's occupation is?" Then the guessing game began."A clerk," said one. "A labourer," said another, "A dockyard worker," said a third and so on. "Well," said the specialist, "what are you?" "I'm a Minister of the Crown and a Member of Parliament." Collapse of stout party, as *Punch* in former days might have observed.

On another occasion he took his battleship through the Skeggs - apparently a very risky operation, and he said that without doubt there would be about a dozen retired admirals monitoring the event and half would be writing to the Admiralty criticizing the way he had hazarded his ship and the other half saying what a fine thing it was that the Navy still had a young captain with a bold and adventurous spirit. Apparently, it was so.

He was a fund of stories - such as the evening Anthony Eden at the time of Suez looking ashen after one of his weekly audiences with the Queen. Apparently he had given his account and had been shattered when the Queen had said, "That is not what my Prime Minister of Canada tells me."

So far as I was concerned, I used to wear a homburg, popularised by Anthony Eden and known by his name as such. I was so disturbed by the events of Suez that I threw it away (in my best "Pooterish" fashion) and started to wear a bowler which I still do: it seemed to me that the Suez adventure should never have been started, or once it had (after all the bungling and delays so reminiscent of the Dardanelles' fiasco 35 years before) it should have been continued. It demonstrated all too clearly that the British Empire had been a creation aided by the use of mirrors.

Jock should have written his own memoirs.

* * * * *

After Jock's first stroke, he lay in intensive care at the hospital and was very unhappy, over little things such as having "Mr" and not "Admiral", on the name pad over his bed. Jean phoned the then Parliamentary Secretary to the Navy (Peter Kirk) whom fortunately she knew and got Jock removed to the Naval Hospital at Haslar.

* * * * *

I entertained someone from my headquarters to luncheon in a restaurant in Chichester; for the reason that follows, I will not name it. He studied the menu, and saw the item, "crepe suzette". The price was high, and he had the courtesy to ask me whether he could order it. Of course, I agreed, but I knew the head waiter would wish to prepare and serve this with due ceremony. Since at 2.10 no trolley had emerged from the recesses of the hotel kitchens, I left my guest to it as I was expecting an important call back in the office at 2.30. The next day I asked the waiter the reason for the quite inordinate delay. He told me. He had gone into the kitchen and ordered what was required, and the chef dropped down dead.

* * * * *

I saw oysters on the menu - a rarity indeed for Chichester. But I was not mindful of my late father's advice: always have them opened in front of you and if they didn't crack, leave them alone, unless it is somewhere like Wheelers' or Scotts used to selling them. Well, this hotel was not - and I really thought my last hour had come, as I was so ill. Never again - for once a bad oyster, you can never eat a good one. I tried on two subsequent occasions - in London in places which were used to oysters - I felt I would die, so it is true - one bad oyster, and that is your lot. Hotels can be dangerous places.

That bowler. It seems to promote so much comment, yet when I was first elected to the Garrick, for example, there were always about eight or 10 other bowlers on adjoining pegs; now mine seems to be the only one. Taxi drivers make gratutious remarks such as "I wish I'd seen you last week; had an American aboard who wanted to see a Britisher actually wearing one." I go to a memorial service in the Temple, and, after taking my name "Q.C., isn't it, Sir", and of course being admitted to the Law Courts without having to explain my mission or my identity, being greeted by a cheerful "Good morning Judge." And at the House of Lords when I was handing in a package of proofs (but it could have been a bomb), for a learned Law Lord who was to write a Foreword, "Let me have that, my Lord. I'll see his Lordship gets it." And all because I thought Anthony Eden had let us down over Suez and that I had literally thrown away my homburg.

And I must not forget Chichester Railway station, where a young booking clerk had, with his colleagues, watched me cross the forecourt and, as he served me with a ticket (it was in the afternoon, and very quiet), said, "We were saying that you are our only customer who wears a bowler." "I wonder why that is?" I said and he replied, "Well, it's as dead as the do do." I drew myself up. "Young man," I said (although in truth he's probably just about to retire), "I'll have you know that once upon a time, I was chairman of the Wild Birds Committee of the West Sussex County Council, and had I been around at the time of the do do - it would have been perfectly safe with me, as a protected species." So there. Although I must add a postscript - the do do had the last laugh on the County Council, because it too is now extinct. All right, the present one occupies the same offices and calls itself the same name - but they cannot fool me, and I am clinging to my bowler hat whatever they say.

A rather 'fraudulent' picture of Barry Rose - I gave up smoking when I was 32, and never, ordinarily, wear a cravat - but as many people compared me to Winston Churchill, including a cab driver in New York who refused to accept a fare. "You look like Mr. Churchill, you speak like Mr. Churchill - nah, I'm not going to accept a fare from you" the picture is included for fun, to see if there is any real likeness!

Some time later, I was travelling down the Mall, and my driver leaned across to speak to another cabbie alongside, whom he obviously knew, and said, "Got Mr. Churchill aboard." Later in the journey, I recounted my New York experience, and my London cabbie said in a kindly fashion, "If you think I'm going to give you a free ride, you have another thought coming!"

And now bowlers of a different kind. Jack Young, England and Middlesex - a raconteur of cricket of rare quality - was hugely proud of having played for England - and once produced for me in the Long Room at Lords a very tattered letter, tattered I suspect as a result of having produced for inspection many times before, signed "Norfolk", ordering him to report for practice. The Duke at the time the letter was written, was Manager of England and was regarded as a hero by Jack.

Jack once told me that he reckoned he was the first to play in a helmet - it was his benefit year, and the rain had been more than normally unkind; he was playing at the Arsenal ground, and just before he went out to face the demon bowler of the day, he "borrowed", on the spur of the moment, a fireman's helmet from its peg at the entrance to the tunnel. It went down well with the crowd. I mention it here as I believe a piece of cricketing history not previously recorded.

* * * * *

I forget his name, but he was a bus conductor (he was also secretary to the Bognor Labour Party). He told me once that he had been brought up in an orphanage in Bristol; it was run by a man who acted upon the principle "The Lord will provide." It was supported entirely by charity, and one day all the children were sitting down waiting hungrily for their food; nothing was in the larder and no food was on the table.

He told the children to pray, himself leading the prayers - a moment's silence, and there was a knock on the door and a man entered, bearing the gift of some food. "Funny, wasn't it?" was his observation to me.

* * * * *

R.O. Dunlop was a Royal Academician who had a studio in Chichester. He was of mixed Scottish/Irish blood. "A bad mixture," he once observed philosophically, and sure enough, he was asked never to darken the doors of a number of pubs in the Chichester area. We became good friends and at one stage in my career I bought a journal called *Art Quarterly* from him.

However, the very strange behaviour of his wife - who once telephoned me seven times before 9 o'clock one Sunday morning (I had to ask the telephone operator in the days when it was actually possible to *talk* to such people, to stop any more calls being put through). She seemed to have an obsession about my wife, somehow getting hold of her telephone number before her marriage to me, and also the belief that I was a rich and opulent tycoon making a fortune out of her husband's genius. To stop the incessant calls, I had to end publication of *Art Quarterly*.

Dunlop told me that if ever he said so much as good morning to me, she would worm it out of him and make his life a misery. As a result I dared not talk to him at all as this would otherwise result in a fresh onslaught - he said she had cost him so many friends but that she had given him two lovely children. However, before I bought *Art Quarterly* (and in the process, by closing it down when I did, losing money I could ill afford) I enjoyed his company enormously.

He told me of his visits to the Astor household - apparently, years before, he had been appointed "unofficial artist" to the Astor family which necessitated visits from time to time to Cliveden. A footman would greet him with decanters containing various alcoholic beverages in the entrance hall; another would unpack his case (consisting of barely more than a change of pair of socks) and would note his alcoholic requirements. He (Dunlop) noticed everything - for example, that Nancy, Lady Astor (then the country's most vocal teetotaller) drank Dubonnet at luncheon; when he taxed her with this, she said it was non-alcoholic. As I recollect - Winston Churchill would never argue with Nancy Astor, and I don't suppose Dunlop would have dared to have done so, either.

I seem to occupy a lot of space discussing alcohol when talking of Dunlop; however, as an artist he was a true professional; in bitterly cold weather, for example, he would paint Arundel Castle and in the process get so carried away by what he was doing he would get frostbite. So he would have been similarly dedicated at Cliveden or anywhere else.

One final story concerning Dunlop - one day we were both discussing the dreadful journeys we had to make to get to London (we didn't know how lucky we were then - the journey was about 15 minutes shorter and we had a restaurant car of blessed memory!) and of the boredom between appointments. He had to go to the Royal Academy quite frequently, and I had a brainwave.

While he was killing time, I suggested, and as he would be in London anyway, could he not go to the Royal Courts of Justice and each time draw for the *J.P.* a cartoon of a Judge - naturally, in the Judge's private chambers and naturally a serious and not "jokey" cartoon?

Mindful as ever of the limitations of my brief for the *J.P.*, I thought it wise to get the assent of Emery, my managing director, to what would be a new departure. As for cost, after some friendly bargaining with Dunlop, I suggested (and he accepted) £4.00 per cartoon. This I thought would be a good promotional idea for the *J.P.* - the Judges I thought would (for the most part) react favourably to be drawn by an eminent RA. The point of the exercise, for the uninitiated, was a promotional one for the *J.P.* -

become a subscriber to the *J.P.* and get the series of cartoons, free, for office decoration. Emery, it must be remembered - was a chartered accountant, and not a publisher, and he thought it would be beyond *his* brief, so he went to see *his* chairman - the Earl of Rothes, (who also was not a publisher, but an engineer) and someone who had been brought in to give "respectability" to the Butterworth Board after the Quennell (*q.v.*)/Maxwell (*q.v.*) episodes.

Emery explained to me later that *he* thought it would be a good promotional idea for the then ailing *Law Times* (subsequently merged with the then ailing *Law Journal* before the merger to make it the successful *New Law Journal*) which had not been my idea at all. Ah, well.

However, to continue, Rothes agreed in principle but said Dunlop must draw Emery first as a "sample" - it would never do if the cartoons pictured the Judges in an unfavourable light and caused them to be "anti-Butterworths" (the owners of the *J.P.*) as a result. As it happens, I know many High Court Judges, but never one failing a sense of humour. Rothes saw the cartoon of Emery, and said, apparently, "You're not as bad as that, Emery," and went on to say what a tragedy it was that someone like Dunlop, an RA, would be prepared to do work like that for £4.00 a time; anyway, the project was dropped. Dunlop said to me subsequently he had only agreed to do the cartoons for me as a friend, he hadn't had any intention of getting involved with big business. Some years before we became friends, he had painted a portrait of me (I must say at a considerably higher fee!) which hangs to this day at home, and I must say (in my opinion) he does not flatter - but everyone else seems to like it. He himself seemed pleased with his cartoon of Emery. "Got him to a T, Barry." Naturally, I do not know what has happened to it since - perhaps, like Sutherland's portrait of Winston

Churchill, it was put to the torch: after all, it only cost £4.00.

* * * * *

When I first started travelling to London regularly at the end of the War, there was a proper restaurant car - owned by the Pullman Company. It was crowded, and so far as I could see, must have been profitable. With nationalization, it took a nosedive and I felt so sorry for the stewards who regarded their "regulars" as friends. I was talking to one steward, and he told me that on the change-over, they were even ordered that they should no longer put a leaf or sprig of parsley on sandwiches, which previously they had done just to make the sandwich look more attractive. On denationalization, what was left of a truncated service (restaurant cars on the last trains, etc., had long since gone) became (as today) a trolley service, so that nowadays we travel surrounded by litter created by earlier passengers and indeed by oneself. It is hardly an improvement. From Dover soles, beef steaks and a selection of wines to a packet of crisps and a tin of lager represents quite a drop in standards, and one wonders if the directors of these companies ever travel by train to experience what they inflict on others.

* * * * *

One of my "early" friends was Col. Alfred Hacking (who lived in Selsey) a solicitor, a member of the Chichester R.D.C.. He was also a director of a railway, the Selsey Tram (*q.v.*). (I do not know where the "colonel" came from.) The tram operated between Chichester and Selsey. Hacking carried with him a medallion establishing his identity and association with the Tram (upon which I myself once travelled as a child), and told me its possession meant he was allowed to travel free on any railway in the world - a courtesy extended between directors of railways. I have no doubt he was too honest to have used it anywhere, for the railway for all practical purposes, had ceased to exist in 1936.

For years in Selsey, people had to put up with "This is Station Road. Where is the station?" before ultimately the local authority was persuaded to change its name; for Terminus Road, at the other end, in Chichester, the name remains the same - an industrial estate is there now, and I cannot help feeling that Terminus has a sound of doom about it. Much better bring back the railway.

Alfred Hacking introduced me to Geddes of the Axe fame; for younger readers, Geddes was not some crazed individual who went round chopping off heads; his Axe was so called for the measures he used in the Great Depression of the 1930s, one of which caused a mutiny in the Royal Navy. A mild and civilized man, I am sure undeserving of the brickbats he attracted.

* * * * *

Before I leave Selsey, I would just like to mention another solicitor - J.A. Allen, who lived in some style in that village, and who used the Selsey Tram every day to get to Chichester, where he would catch the Victoria train. He was solicitor to the Westminster city council (although not employed by it) and his firm at that time were, I believe, also parliamentary agents and they probably still are. He also maintained a substantial household in London itself. I was offered his diaries for publication covering every day of the Great War and found it, personally, interesting almost beyond belief. Alas, it required a much heavier investment than I could have made - also, as a law publisher, we did not have the marketing skills necessary for such a work - but the Diaries are simply crying out to be published and I do so hope his family may be made an offer.[1] He was a polymath - for example, he made violins; he wrote books and lectured on palmistry on both sides of the Atlantic (from about 1906 onwards) but read his daughter's hand when a child and forecast that she would die a violent death when between 22 and 23 (he pinned the reading - in, I believe, 1906 - to a newspaper dated the day of the palm reading; she was killed at the forecast age in a car accident when an undergraduate at Oxford; thereafter, he stopped this particular activity and involved himself in a whole host of other things).

To me the Diaries were the most fascinating part of this treasure trove. They were in my hands for a relatively short period, and I am speaking purely from memory without being able to refresh it - but I recall, for example, his entry at the beginning of the War in 1914, when he demanded some money in gold from the local bank, which refused to give it to him and offered notes as it was the policy of the Government to withdraw gold from circulation.

After much argument on the illegality of such an action, he got his gold. Professor Bryan Harvey of Birmingham University, a lawyer who also makes violas as a hobby, came across Allen's other work in this field and got in touch with me as a publisher he knew. I had no idea making violas was such a nerve-wracking and intricate business. I took Harvey and his wife (who had edited the Diaries) to the Garrick, where naturally, Allen had been a member for many years until his death in 1941 (I say naturally, because Allen seems to pop up in every direction). The West Sussex County Archivist, Richard Childs, regards him as one of his department's major finds for the last (20th) century.

---

1.   I see from the *Chichester Observer* for August 16, 2002, that Phillimore has published a book on Allen and the First World War, at £20.00.

When William Ewart Gladstone inspired the creation of parish councils in the 1890s, he would have had little idea of how this would work in practice. Of course, there was (as there still is) antipathy between town and country - the townies who come to the country, and want street lighting, no noises from, say, cows giving birth, no farmyard smells, and metalled roads and all the appurtenances of modern civilisation whilst at the same time retaining the natural beauty of the countryside provided, of course, there are no flocks of sheep on the roads, or anything else likely to inconvenience the incomers. Those incomers. Ah yes - when they came to the village of Pagham they brought with them the entirely erroneous belief that parish councils were the same as borough councils or even county borough councils, and had their own powers and were not constricted by statute to act in most respects through either the (then) rural district council or the county council. Therefore, one of the first things to do was to found a ratepayers' association, and to get control of the parish council and see what these people were up to. The sitting council was somewhat wounded to think that their management of the council was being questioned in this way; thus, it came about that it resolved to ignore the threat - the general feeling was that when, say, the siting of a postbox meant writing to the Post Office for their help in this respect, it hardly needed a galvanizing force such as a ratepayers' association to direct their activities. So, nobly, the existing council gritted their collective teeth, and decided to ignore this threat from the incomers.

One member of the council - possibly the most well-known member - had the best of personal reasons for wishing to lie low during the election period. It was not a Miss Lewinsky/President Clinton situation, but nevertheless it was a matter which, understandably, he wished to keep quiet in the wholly mistaken belief that by so doing, the whole parish would not know about it.

Poor fellow, he let it be known that he wished not to stand, as he was too busy on other things, but was assured that he was so badly needed on the parish council, and in effect, was talked out of retiring from that august body and was persuaded to stand again. But the parish council members decided that none of them would fight as individuals to these incomer chaps; and that a single dignified statement of the work that they, collectively, had done for the past umpteen years would suffice to persuade the electorate that now was not the time for change.

A joker then entered the pack. Someone from the neighbouring urban district of Bognor Regis who knew nothing of the inner workings of the parish, decided that his friend - the unwilling candidate - was never going to win the election by standing aloof like this - so it must be surmised that partly as a joke and partly out of genuine concern that unless he (the friend of the unwilling candidate) put some gumption in the campaign, his friend would lose his seat.

Therefore, without the candidate's knowledge, far less than with his consent, at six o'clock in the morning or even earlier on the day of election, this chap went round with a pot of gum and dozens of posters extolling his friend's virtues - who, as I say, had had the best of reasons for wishing to keep his candidature as low key as possible - and fly-posting these throughout the whole parish, including the polling booth itself; and these described him as a ratepayers' candidate for good measure. It will be seen at once that this course of action would have the very reverse effect to that intended: to the fellow members of the parish council, it seemed a betrayal of his colleagues by sending out such a message for himself whereas they had all decided to stand united against the common foe; the ratepayers' association could not hide their indignation that someone who had not been selected by them, was stealing their unblemished reputation and standing as one of their chosen candidates. So far as the majority of the parish was concerned, well, after what he had done, you would have thought he would have had a little shame and would keep quiet for a bit, but look at him - all this blatant advertising for himself. Almost as bad as the incomers.

The Returning Officer arrived at the Polling Booth (I think in those days it opened at 2 p.m.) - saw it plastered with "Vote For ..." notices, and immediately ordered their removal. But who was to remove them? The candidate said he had not put them up, so he was not going to take them down. The posters did not say who was responsible for the printing of the notices, and who was the electoral agent, and so on, in defiance of election law. Big trouble looming: who were the perpetrators? And where were they to be found?

And where was the candidate himself? By this time, he was nowhere to be seen, and it later emerged he had on the admirable principle of discretion being the better part of valour, left the parish to stay with relatives in a far-off town. He was not therefore present when the returning officer declared the results later in the evening; not surprisingly, he was bottom of the poll.

* * * * *

Norman (now Lord) Tebbitt - when chairman of the Conservative Party, received a letter from me saying (and providing details) that I had signed up for membership of the Conservative Party three Labour Party parliamentary candidates. Was this a record? I asked.

With commendable economy of words, he replied, "Probably, but to make sure, make it four."

* * * * *

In Selsey on the South Coast there is a swathe of land beginning with East Beach Selsey, Pagham Harbour, Pagham Lagoon, Pagham East and West Beach and Church Farm Pagham. An estate of considerable value - yet two solicitors separately involved in the estate committed suicide, and the owner died in protection virtually bankrupt. I was personally offered as many acres of East Beach, Selsey as I wanted, at 10 shillings an acre, but "I'd better warn you," with a smile, "that it is under the sea at present." Thus Jack Gates, senior partner of Wyatts, in the days when estate agents were *estate* agents. Nevertheless, I think it would be fair to say that for others - ie, I had no pecuniary interest in such matters, I was instrumental for the purchase of Pagham Harbour (of which more later); Pagham Lagoon, Pagham West Beach (and Pagham East Beach, with J.P. Shaw, a resident and an accountant, from a different owner) in all of which I had no personal stake nor received any personal reward other than as a resident of the area; in other words, I was not involved for business reasons nor sought any pecuniary advantage.

The owner (see above) of Pagham Church Farm had let the farm - I imagine usual agricultural tenancy - but as a War was on, an organisation came into being - the War Agricultural Committee, which had power to transfer the tenancy and do everything else to ensure maximum food production. Which, in wartime, was fair enough. Nowhere has the role of these committees, not only in West Sussex, but country-wide, been examined in depth, but in a local context, Church Farm, Pagham, like every other farm, came under the aegis of such a committee (which, on the whole, consisted of local farmers and landowners). The farmer in this case, Cyril Dutton, had gone to War as a member of the Sussex Yeomanry, leaving his wife and five adult daughters to run the farm, a task of which they were more than capable, bearing in mind that as it was so close to the sea, and not suitable for ploughing, because the chalk was just under the surface and that they had been running it not unsuccessfully for five years. It should be said as will be apparent that the farm was hardly sustainable consisting as it did of the house, some farm buildings, and a couple of fields - most of the farm was some distance away.

The War over, and Cyril Dutton returned to Church Farm when one evening he answered the door to be confronted by the much younger neighbouring farmer Bernard Hender, who had not gone to the War, and who had entered the parish in West Sussex from East Sussex. As recounted to me, by one of the daughters, Hender stood on the doorstep (at about 7 p.m.) and said to Dutton, "Sorry about this, Cyril, but I'm the new tenant." There had been no previous warning.

The swingeing powers of the War Agricultural Committee, possessing unprecedented powers in peacetime, had transferred the tenancy presumably on the grounds that the land was not being farmed productively.

And that was that. But then (as I heard from the lips of the then wife of the "new" tenant at Church Farm), one evening in the summer of 1947 or 1948 a stranger knocked on the door, and asked permission to park his caravan for a night under some trees in the fore distance (she was describing to me with her hands the actual spot). She had hesitated, and the caravan owner added, "I'll give you 10 bob [50 pence]." That clinched it; the very next night, another stranger called, with exactly the same request. Ten shillings was not an inconsiderable amount in those days - therefore, when thinking of enlargement, and development as a caravan park, the date became one of some importance - was it before or after June 30, 1948? - for this was the date when the Town and Country Planning Act 1947 came into operation. Was the land being used as farm land or as a caravan site on the appointed day? But there were other factors. For example, before the War, some Boy Scouts used to camp on the land. Did this establish previous use? And not all the land was Church Farm - an adjoining landowner (initially, probably the Ecclesiastical Commissioners) came into the picture. Certainly it was complicated, and I was not of course privy to those matters outside the public sector or which have been vouchsafed to me in - if you like - gossip from an informed source. The first Mrs. Hender told me that when the second 10s was handed over, she thought for the first time, "there's money in this". Indeed, yes. It became, according to the *Sunday Times*, the second largest site in Europe, worth of course a lot of money (although I suspect the owners of the Estate got precious little out of it, its value calculated not perhaps as a caravan site, but as agricultural land, although here I am probably wrong).

As for the residents of the area - they were (apart from the tiny minority who obtained jobs as a result of the site) not best pleased - it had grown so fast there were few facilities (and because the site was so close to the sea it was so popular anyway and the demand so great that there was no desperate need or urgency on the part of the owner to get them) so that when I, as the newly elected member of the Chichester R.D.C. went to the site, I was struck (at a distance) by what appeared to be two black, fairly thick, magic carpets hovering in the air at the side of the field. I truly had no idea what they were, but as I approached, I perceived they were flies. They were coping with the sewage of the site, deposited in two large holes in the ground.

Naturally the officers of the authority (Chichester R.D.C.) did their damnedest to improve matters (but of course they had problems in other parishes) and one neighbour to the site accused me of accepting "bribes" in allowing the situation. Ultimately I appeared at County Hall before the Agricultural Committee to make my protest. (A long time later I was told that Mr. Hender's then brother-in-law was a member of the Agricultural Committee - although of course I do not know if he took part in the deliberations affecting Church Farm or even whether he was actually present at the meeting - he was a farmer who ran a highly successful caravan site seven or eight miles away.) After all, I said, the tenant had been summarily dismissed because presumably his land was not producing sufficient food: now it was producing no food at all. I was treated with every courtesy, but was told that the Government had laid down guidelines - that due to the currency difficulties people could not go abroad for their holidays and therefore every effort had to be made to accommodate them at home. Yet somehow the memory of the honourable resignation of the then Minister of Agriculture, Sir Thomas Dugdale, and the image of Commander Marten, and Crichel Down, will not go away. I am told that the shock of being informed, on the doorstep of his house, that Cyril Dutton was no longer tenant of the farm he had in effect gone to War about, was responsible for his subsequent and early death.

Anyway, after my meeting with the Agriculture Committee, frustrated and baffled, I returned to Pagham; there, I continued to be the recipient of further complaints - one a particularly poignant one - from someone who had to leave to catch the early train from Bognor to London each morning; a night club had opened up in the caravan "headquarters" almost immediately opposite his house. Although licensing hours were only until 10.30, the noise of doors slamming would - he alleged - continue sometimes until 1 a.m. or even later.

So I took this complaint to the parish council; that particular evening, there was no press, and no public (not because they had not been informed but presumably because they had better things to do and kept away) so thus, in the event, seemingly in deep secrecy, we hatched a plot: the chairman (a farmer from the other end of the parish and one who had no interest in caravans or "caravan farming") and I had a meeting with the Chief Constable at the request of the parish council. (By this time a former councillor from Croydon County Borough, no less - a Mrs. Hilda Bunning - was beginning to make her presence felt in the parish, but, as can be imagined, fitted into parish affairs as was then constituted, like a square peg into a round hole and was a woman to boot! But all things change, and development was proceeding at a very rapid pace; she subsequently succeeded me on the rural and county councils; however, she did not attend this particular meeting.)

The Chief Constable - a nice chap called Col. Paterson Wilson - agreed to our request; he was to order a raid on the said premises for the following Friday evening.

So, the following Friday evening, those of us in the know were agog - but all was as silent as a grave in the area of the club; stories in due course percolated down, and we discovered that customers had had to pack up and be away with lights switched off by 10.15 or thereabouts, and when, at 10.40 the police pounced, the place was in darkness.

Well, there was no point in asking the Chief Constable to organise a second raid. Weeks later, the local Police constable stopped his bicycle in the village street and spoke to me about it. He said his colleagues at headquarters had 'phoned him about the impending raid. "Well, I went along to see Bernard Hender, and warned him what was to happen. Well, I didn't want headquarters to intervene on my patch, did I? But who tipped them off? I reckon it was that Mrs. Bunning, can't think of anyone else likely to do so."

Oh dear. Poor Mrs. Bunning. And craven me in not owning up.

But as icing on the cake, just two further pieces. Hender, the farmer, told me that he was approached by two men for the purchase of two derelict farm cottages - I said yes, but warned them they would not get planning consent for rebuilding as I had already applied for it and been turned down. They bought the cottages and went ahead, and I saw them working on them at weekends. Then some months later I discovered they were both in the planning department at County Hall. (In those days there was no statutory requirement for all planning applications to be published.) The cottages now appear as very pleasant additions to the landscape. But ...?

And finally, I saw a senior employee of the County Agricultural Committee leave Church Farm one evening just before the Christmas holiday with a brace of pheasants. When he saw me I thought he seemed just a little disconcerted: I suspect he knew the inference I would draw from such a sighting.

Of course, this long and rambling tale is an imperfect one. I can only recount what was said, what I heard, read and saw, and reasoned, but I think it makes an interesting little tale over a matter affecting the lives of many - in today's world, of course, it could not happen like that, as a result of statutory safeguards, and the Planning Act of 1947 was in effect the predecessor of all the regulation that has followed.

And when Bernard Hender died, the local paper referred to him as 'Squire of Pagham' - so he's all right, then.

* * * * *

Sadly, I regard myself as one of the most determined of the Nimby Brigade - perhaps not entirely true, but I suppose I am more conservative than is good for me, for my blood pressure always rises when anything affecting wild life or indeed anything relating to the wild places, is at risk, and in Pagham there is the most glorious of wild places in West Sussex - Pagham Harbour.

Whilst I have nothing against caravans or caravan site owners - Pagham in the early 1950s had, in my opinion, more than its fair share; at that particular time, planning control was in its infancy (lack of trained staff was one reason). Therefore, planning control did not really begin to affect the population in 1948, following passing the Bill of the previous year - incidentally it was said during the course of the Parliamentary Debates that only two people in the House really understood what the Bill was all about - Lewis Silkin, the Minister who piloted it through the House, and David Kilmuir, his opposite number. Thus it seemed more than likely that something would happen in the planning process where the local view would be over-ridden by legal technicalities.

Pagham Harbour was (so I was told at the time) visited by no fewer than 330 species of birds (although not all at once!) and 'twitchers' came from far and wide to photograph and just to look. (There were others - shooters, who were to claim special rights over the Harbour.)

Therefore, hearing this completely unsubstantiated rumour (and even I, slow-witted as I am, realised that had I asked Hender (*q.v.*) as to its veracity, if not, fine, but afterwards he could easily change his mind once the idea had been planted in it), I resolved something must be done.

My own experiences of the Harbour were limited to my very short war time service in the Home Guard, when we used the old Salt Hut on the edge of the Harbour; very occasionally, on a wild and stormy night, a mine would explode as a particularly heavy wave would smash onto the shore. In the blackness, not even seeing the flash, it was rather alarming. But all was peaceful in the years after the war, and now was this rumour that the Harbour was to became a floating caravan park (please do not laugh at the quaint phraseology; a more fashionable noun such as houseboat doubtless would be more appropriate). I want to emphasize again it was only a rumour - but we all know that rumours can be harbingers of actuality. It seemed all too reasonable to suppose that Mr. Hender, the owner of the adjoining caravan site, as a result of the unbounded success of that site, would now have all the funds needed to develop the Harbour if he wished so to do; planning controls were so weak that if he made a determined effort, he would succeed. Undoubtedly in a planning context, to establish prior use to the coming into force of the 1947 Planning Act (Commencement date July 1, 1948), he could readily have found people who could say, truthfully, that they had, prior to the coming into force of the Act, slept in their launches in the Harbour when cruising round the coast, and one way and another, this tranquil part of Pagham would be gone for ever.

Therefore, what was to be done? The owner was, I believed, a sick man and his wife seemed to be ailing; the large estate which included the Harbour was in trusteeship; the chief trustee lived in Lancashire. I made contact with him, and he (in my opinion) very decently came down to London to meet me. Yes, he would be prepared to sell the Harbour and quoted a very reasonable price: of course, I had no thought of owning it myself, and I approached all the amenity associations I could think of, such as the National Trust, the RSPB and so on with the idea that perhaps they could take it over as a nature reserve/bird sanctuary.

They all replied in the negative, but I was determined to plough on - most were sympathetic for an idea of a bird sanctuary; some pleaded lack of funds; some that they were not empowered by their founding statutes, but I was determined to continue in the hope that some organisation somewhere would be interested. And then a chap called Michael Ordish from the local "Observer" Group of local newspapers phoned me. Poor fellow, he had been struck down by polio in his 20s or early 30s, and continued as a journalist relying upon the 'phone. Every so often he would telephone me for news of anything happening, and rather stupidly I told him what I was attempting over Pagham Harbour, but with the caveat that at present it was all under wraps, but I would let him know immediately I was able to report something positive. But so far as he was concerned, it was *not* under wraps; once I had told him, it was in the public arena and of course from that moment, my patient plodding through the list of amenity associations, one by one hoping to find one with money to spare, came to a juddering halt. I am not being critical of Ordish - he was quite right.

I had been a member of the county council for about two years by this time, and the appropriate officer as a result of the publicity approached me, and suggested that because of liability for coast protection charges (likely to be quite excessive, he thought), it would make sense for the county council to buy it, and thus bring it into public ownership. The wild fowlers now also came into the act: they claimed special rights over the Harbour (quite speciously, in my opinion) but I knew it would not be long before other people had ideas about the Harbour - if not for a Marina then for some other aquatic purpose - and of course I knew that if they came in with a higher bid, the Trustees would (all things being equal) be bound to accept it. Therefore, I accepted, and passed over the documentation to the County Council who took it on from there. I confess to being disappointed when an official of the county council suggested that part of the land adjoining the harbour be sold off, which, he said, would more than pay off its cost. *That* had not been my idea at all, and thereafter I dropped out of Harbour matters.

The county council rewarded me (or at least, that is what it looked like) with a committee chairmanship - the Wild Birds Committee (which I do not think lasted for much longer - but the officers impressed me enormously with the amount of accumulated information they had on the Harbour).

* * * * *

A friend of mine, who shall be nameless in relation to what I have to say - took someone he knew - (as it happens, it was Mr. Jinnah, generally credited as being the Founder of Pakistan) to Lincoln's Inn. My friend is even older than I, but one of the practices of the Bar was that in addition to passing exams, you had to eat a certain number of dinners at your Inn (a practice being phased out). The dining arrangements were generally tables of four - with two bottles of wine per table. Mr. Jinnah, a Muslim (and, as I understand it, before Pakistan became independent) had never drunk alcohol - and although to most people in England, the equivalent of half a bottle of wine, accompanied by food, would have had, I would have thought, negligible effect: to Mr. Jinnah, however, it was different and he was apparently rendered legless. My friend tells me that he emptied his pockets of all his private valuables, such as wallet, watch, money etc. and inserted a card in his pocket telling him where they were to be found in the morning, so that he would know he had not been robbed; a taxi summoned, and told to take him home. I often heard of the 'dining in term' and how Bar students so wanted to have a table shared with a Moslem or preferably two, so that their share of the wine would be greater! But he, Mr. Jinnah, obviously took his own proper share - with, on this occasion, disastrous results.

* * * * *

At one time, and for some time, I was known, says he with unbecoming modesty, as the "uncrowned king" of Pagham. The postman would deliver letters to me which addressed to the "tourist and guides office" (Pagham had none); the Mayor of Pagham (Pagham had none); and to the Town Clerk (Pagham had none) and to a number of other offices I did not possess - but I *was* the county councillor and the rural councillor and chairman of this and chairman of that and president of the other. (Oddly, and for a peculiar reason, I was, simultaneously, even Chairman, Treasurer and Secretary of the old Pagham Village Hall!) But it will be appreciated if there was one thing I did not want to be - it was a parish councillor. Already, in my other councillorships, the parish council had to approach me - which gave me a position of some (mostly illusory) power. Once, however, I became a member of the parish council, I became one of "them", and my power such as it was, became diluted.

Of course, I had always been prepared to attend meetings - but I was then in the position of being able to attend their meetings almost as a favour - but as a member I ran the risk of allowing some other parish councillor know that my seat on the parish council was tenuous - so that in the popularity stakes, if you like, I might come some way down in the number of votes cast, compared with my colleagues, one of whom might thus feel tempted to challenge me at the next election for the Chichester rural council or for the West Sussex county council. I mention this merely to emphasise that "Please, mister, I didn't want to be a member. Honest."

But I gave way. The Clerk said the parish council would gain so much in prestige etc., with me as a member. Well, those of us who can resist temptation are certainly caught by flattery. So I stood, and as it happened topped the poll on every subsequent occasion.

First, it was a rural community and the parish council reflected this - those serving were the baker, the publican (oddly, a crew survivor from the Titanic, who told me once that the lifeboat he had been ordered to row, was half empty), the professional man, the farmer, the butcher, the farmer's son, and one vacancy. There was no woman member of the council - that would have been unthinkable, for it was plainly a man's job.

Alas, man's job it may have been, but the poor Clerk (a solicitor) found himself on trial for the usual offences in relation to clients' monies, and was sent down for (I believe) 12 months. His defence was that he had been blackmailed ever since his honeymoon - for what he never explained, but when he came out of prison he said to me he was happier than at any previous time of his life. But as the parish council had paid him his fees a year in advance, in order that no extra cost would fall on the ratepayers, or risking surcharges on the members. I became for that one year honorary Clerk myself.

Which reminds me. When I first became a member of the Chichester R.D.C., the Clerk was a delightful man, incidentally without any professional qualifications; he had begun as an office boy in the former Westhampnett rural council before it had been merged into Chichester R.D.C. Naturally, today such a person would never even have 'made' the short list, but it will be appreciated that what he did not know about the district and those who represented it, was just not worth knowing.

Leonard Bailey (a bachelor) was in effect father to his members - stopped them getting into trouble and was also father to the parish councils forming part of the rural council. He told me that over my own parish, Pagham, the then clerk of that parish council had come to see him and had complained he did not think he was getting a fair salary - £5.00 per annum. (This was either just before the war, or just after it.) No, said Mr. Bailey, it did not seem fair to him either, and he promised to have words with the chairman of the parish council, the next time he saw him. The chairman asked what the clerk would recommend, so Bailey (knowing that the parish council would cut it down - he thought £50.00 would have been a fair figure) suggested £75.00. The chairman of the parish council reported back in due course: the clerk had been ordered outside while the parish council considered his request (it was a cold night in February, and raining: the meeting was held in the cricket pavilion, so for the poor chap there was no cover of any sort) and ultimately he was summoned to be told the council had considered his request, and had decided to increase his wage for the year to £7.50. As told by Leonard Bailey, with mimicry of the chairman (a truly rural farmer), it was joyous theatre.

* * * * *

One of the men I most admired was Andrew Montague-Douglas-Scott - always in fearful pain from a War injury, nevertheless he managed to keep a sparkling sense of fun: when he died, his obituary in *The Daily Telegraph* recounted how, on the Italian Front, he maintained champagne standards even in his foxhole. I never saw him drunk, although I do recall that after swimming in the sea, he would visit the local hostelry, *The Ship* at Aldwick, have a triple double gin and then have a jug of water to wash it down. I recall the landlord, Eric Bailey, telling me that he had decided to relinquish the licence because he could not bear to watch men killing themselves, and I suspect he had Andrew Montague-Douglas-Scott as one of those in mind. It is difficult to recapture the spirit of his wit - but I recall a story which dated back to pre-War, when at a dinner party he found himself using his shirt-tail coming out of his flies as a napkin. (Older readers may reflect upon the huge quantity of material which went into a shirt then; I wonder what has happened to it since?)

* * * * *

I have mentioned the arrival at Chichester of the Earl of Rothes, and of his appearance in my office. He told Emery that he thought the *J.P.* should be renamed (he made the remark facetiously, or at least, I *hope* it was meant facetiously!) *The Bastards' Gazette*. This was because at that time, the Law of Bastardy and Affiliation was not yet a dead duck, and boys and girls who did not behave themselves according to the *mores* of society, found the State on the whole unwilling to fork out for the upkeep of the little bastards who arrived all too regularly nine months later, and the *J.P.* occupied a lot of space dealing with the incredibly complex problems brought about by such behaviour. This was light years away from DNA, and even blood tests were not reliable - letters and indiscreet talk to women friends seemed to be the main basis for determining paternity; yet cumbersome as it may now seem, it did not run up a debt of £2 billion as has the Child Benefit Agency, which the rest of us have to pay for other people's bastards. Legal readers may just remember Lushington's *Law of Affiliation and Bastardy* - there was quite a lot of law about concerning it, and the work ran to many editions; but nowadays in effect the State has given up the unequal struggle of trying to regulate such matters (Lushington had been one of the editors of the *J.P.* for a period in the 19th century). Now apparently the word bastard itself has gone out of fashion - yet it is a good English word which very clearly defines a situation which has been brought about by two people affecting the status of a third, whereas the use of the "F" word is generally used these days as a meaningless exhibition of a poorly equipped vocabulary.

* * * * *

I have been to many Party Conferences, but the one held at Margate is a classic in my memory. I was to make my own hoped-for debut as a conference speaker on the Saturday morning. It was a somewhat unnerving prospect, for the Conservatives then had (they may have still) the largest free political movement in the world, and the arrangement for the annual conference in those days was that throughout the week everyone dealt with the major political problems of the day, but on the Saturday we all prepared for the Leader (who had remained in his hotel suite throughout the week, so that a fever of expectation was created among the delegates) to address us in the afternoon, where he would send us forth into the country rejuvenated and reinvigorated and as a result we would win the next election. That, at any rate, was the theory.

On the Saturday morning, no one took much notice, as whatever was said would be submerged beneath the rhetoric of the Leader in the afternoon, but obviously the time could not be wasted, part of which I was to occupy speaking upon the need for coast protection to be a national, rather than a local, charge. (Today - I am of the opposite opinion - because of climate warming it would be an impossible burden, and one ridiculous to take on board the public sector.)

Well, things did not quite work out as planned. To start with, the Leader was Winston Churchill, and mystery had surrounded him for about two months. The whole Conference had been buzzing with news (a) that he would not deliver the speech at all, (b) that because of ill-health, he would resign the leadership, (c) that he would indicate that Eden was to take over, and so on and so forth. But of course, Dame Rumour had been responsible for all this - hard news was difficult to come by.

As for myself, I was up about half the night rehearsing the speech I was going to make in the morning. Coast protection may not sound the most exciting of subjects, but here I was, with this vast audience, and it was up to me to see that they ate out of my hand. Every syllable had to be enunciated to bring the maximum input; every nuance had to be weighed; every gesture had to be just right - so it was, that through the night I was rehearsing in my hotel bedroom in front of a mirror which I almost wore out. My seconder was to be Air Vice-Marshall Langford-Sainsbury, who was treasurer of the constituency association. So there we were, waiting for our cue, and then Lord Woolton, chairman of the Party, took the rostrum.

The audience went wild with enthusiasm when he announced that Winston - the great Winston - was, after all, going to speak that afternoon. And then he announced that he had been looking at the programme or agenda for that morning; it looked a bit dull, he thought, so he had asked old Conference favourites Dorothy Welfare and Bob Bullbrook, to give a little light relief to the proceedings. Both speakers were wonderful crowd-pleasers. Mrs. Welfare had a string bag, with some groceries, showing what could be bought with a pound note under the Conservatives, and another string bag, showing what little could be bought under Labour. She was tremendously popular with constituencies. Bob Bullbrook was a former trades union enthusiast working for the Gas Board or something similar, and he was able to tell in graphic detail incidents from his former life relating particularly to the trade union movement. But Rose ... those wasted hours in front of the looking glass. Oh dear.

But Langford-Sainsbury was not a man to be cheated. After our disappointment, he and I went out of Margate to a neighbouring village to a place to which he had been recommended in which to eat. He was a big man; some of us who remember him would say a very big man; he had a big appetite and the breathalyser had not yet been invented - we had quite an appreciable amount to eat and to drink and both of us began to think that perhaps the world was not such a bad place after all.

In the afternoon we returned to the hall, which was filling up fast, and sat about two-thirds back. The great Winston - whispered of that morning and the previous few days as being close to death - had private grief that day: his dog Rufus had been killed in a car accident and I have no doubt that as a highly emotional man, he was much affected by it.

Almost immediately, however, once on the platform, we recognised the old Winston magic - he sipped water at the rostrum "You don't see me drinking this stuff very often," and the speech then developed into one of his better ones.

Now I have no doubt that Winston was fairly accustomed to the noise of battle, with bombs dropping out of the sky, with artillery coughing forth, with rifle fire and mortar bombs, with mines and klaxons: yes, he would have known all about the noises of battle, and for him, each speech *was* a battle, against the stupidity of his political friends and the evil of his political foes, etc. But just as his speech was getting into its stride, he paused uncertainly; no, it couldn't be, but yes, most definitely, it was. Someone out there in that great concourse, was actually snoring.

I don't suppose he had heard such a noise ever before in his political life and that noise was emanating from the seat next to mine, and the snore belonged to Langford-Sainsbury.

He was, as I have said, a big man, and his snore was big to match. Brutally, I dug him in the ribs, I pinched him and savagely hit him in the midriff - but the snoring went on and Winston stood silent and perplexed - he probably took another sip of water, although I cannot say for certain: I am sure he just couldn't believe it. About 2000 moon-like faces turned back as in a Bateman cartoon - a most extraordinary sensation for me. Ultimately I was able to wake him, and all returned to normal.

I can tell this story, because he never resented me telling it in his presence years later - and, also years later, at yet another Party Conference (at Brighton, where the then ice-rink had been boarded over for the Conference) I was sitting on a side seat, and one of the great lamps immediately above him burst. In slow motion, I watched the glass descend upon his head and shoulders - to my great admiration, he did not move so much as a muscle as it showered down on his head and shoulders.

And no, he was not asleep *that* time.

* * * * *

A merry morning at Wittering (I forget whether it was east or west of the seaside villages on the outskirts of Chichester - but wherever it was, the twain did indeed meet there for the purposes of a Joint Main Drainage System). The work was now completed, and the consulting engineers invited us to a party (modest, I hasten to say) held at one of the pumping stations.

The consulting engineer, smiling as if to indicate that he did not expect compliance, invited me to inspect the bottom of the inspection pit (or whatever it was called) where a trickle of liquid was beginning to show itself. (One does not inquire too deeply into the nature of such substances). The pit, although only about 12 feet deep, nevertheless seemed pretty formidable for me to descend using the metal steps built into the wall, so I said, as I thought reasonably, that this was a job I was happy to delegate to my vice-chairman - a certain ex-police superintendent Brett. He peered down and announced that he wasn't going down either, and congratulated me on my wisdom in having nothing to do with it. So far, everything was fairly jolly. Then the chairman of the Public Health Committee announced that if I wasn't going down, *he* would, as a matter of public duty. I never knew his Christian name (his surname was Jacques) he was 84, and almost blind - without realising just how close he was to the completely unguarded hole he impulsively (before anyone could stop him) stepped off over the void. As we all caught our breath, so he was caught in mid-air by the contractor.

For his second attempt, the contractor went first down the steps to catch him in case he fell; a silence descended upon the assembly as we listened to this little drama being played out - then we at the top heard a cry followed by a thump - in due course, he re-emerged from the hole covered in what was (presumably) white cement dust - either that, or lime, and I expect he was quite moist from the liquid now gradually accummulating there. To those of us curious about the strangulated cry, the consulting engineer told us later the volunteer had missed the final two or three steps. But our colleague did his duty, and the National Health Service escaped scot-free, it being nothing short of a miracle that no limbs were broken.

* * * * *

Whatever else I may be, I am *not* a business man, yet for a period I had dealings with the great firm of Robert Fleming - in the City of London. Their offices were decidedly not opulent, for that would imply a degree of vulgarity, whereas everything about them spelt class and style. Every four or five months I would be invited to luncheon: possibly with a business meeting before or after - where I was invariably 'in the dark' as to what was going on - I suppose I was literally wet behind the ears in a business sense. In spite of everything, and my tendency to regard everything quite literally, Robert Fleming were unfailingly kind, and Brian Lewis (my 'minder') so unfailingly humorous, that my sister Monica's advice - then a woman executive of one of the 'Big Five' banks - who had said crisply, "Go to Robert Fleming. There's no one else" was 100% correct. But at such luncheons I would find myself with some of the biggest figures in British Industry; one day I found myself sitting next to a colleague of my 'minder' Brian Lewis, called 'Miles'. Otherwise I had no knowledge who he was, but like Brian and all the other people from Robert Fleming, he was utterly charming. "I've so wanted to sit next to you," he said, and asked me to tell him about West Sussex. Subsequently, I discovered that he was a major general, but otherwise I had no idea that he was to be promoted up the genealogical ladder until he became the Duke of Norfolk. I confess I probably would have been a little more guarded in some of my answers to his inquiries, particularly those about the then Duke whom he was to succeed.

* * * * *

Every time I think about Robert Fleming and everyone I met there, including and especially the ever-patient Brian, who many times must have thought he was dealing with a cretin, as in business terms, he certainly was. Although nothing to do with me, I am sorry it has now gone to America - yet, with corporate crime apparently burgeoning in the US, it needs a few firms like Robert Fleming to raise their standards of corporate life.

* * * * *

Walter Stirland, a fellow member (and during my term, latterly my vice-chairman of the Public Services Committee) of the Chichester R.D.C., told me he had started his career as a 14 year-old down the pit, after about a month, he was called out on strike. (This would have been sometime in the late 1920s.) He could not stand idleness, so, while still in his teens, he tendered to build four council houses in Doncaster. He got the job, built the houses, and then walked south, from Doncaster - stopping at farms etc. on the way down, asking for any casual work. He ultimately arrived at Birdham, a village on the outskirts of Chichester, sent a postcard to his girl friend, said he had found it, and she was to come down. It was the Shangri-la for which he had been seeking. He built up a very substantial business, became chairman of the Chichester R.D.C., and had his own cricket team, which continues to this day.

The Conservative Party had clearly marked Stirland out as a person who might be persuaded to contribute more than the odd half-crown and sent down E.R.T. Holmes, the former England and Surrey cricketer, from Conservative Central Office as a fund-raiser. A luncheon was arranged and, as constituency chairman, I was also present to meet Holmes. At an appropriate point in the proceedings, Stirland produced a cheque book, and gave a handsome cheque to Central Office, and one to me for local funds, of the same dimension.

In conversation, it emerged that Holmes and his wife had spent the previous weekend at Arundel Castle, as the guests of the Duke of Norfolk - it would have been for a cricketing purpose, as Prince Philip was President of the M.C.C. and the Duke was Manager of the England side - E.R.T. Holmes was a former Captain; also on that occasion house guests were the Queen and H.R.H. the Duke of Edinburgh. Holmes spoke with wonder at the physical fitness of Prince Philip - who had spent the day racing at Cowes; had arrived by helicopter at the Castle at about eleven at night, and then played snooker until three in the morning. Holmes had been invited to discuss cricket.

I heard once - and there is some credence for the truth of this story - that for a match when Sussex and Hampshire played at the Priory Park Ground in Chichester. The Sussex team supporters entertained the Hampshire side so well that the following morning

Hampshire in the field performed, shall we say, disappointingly, and the Duke as President said the Priory Park Ground was never again to be used for such matches. Well, it may be a coincidence, but I don't recall a county game there since, although I confess I have never researched the matter.

* * * * *

I am a great admirer of Edward du Cann. Part of the reason is personal - when my own political career - although technically, it was hardly ever in a state of development to have justified such grandiose phraseology, was plainly in tatters having just lost the Chichester nomination to Christopher Chataway (who, quite apart from being a nice personable chap, was then in the glory of having been pacemaker for Roger Bannister's epoch-making four minute mile, and former newscaster on *News at Ten*, apart from having been a former Member of Parliament for one of the Lewisham seats which he had lost at the earlier General Election, and a strikingly handsome man). Of course, I was not in the race at all - quite apart from Chris's speech (which of course I did not hear) which was said by those who *did* hear it and in particular by Peter Fleck (*q.v.*) who subsequently told me it was brilliant. I gave a particularly pathetic performance - a truly dreadful speech, when even now, I squirm at the recollection, and apologise to my own supporters for letting them down; although of course Chris would have won anyway. However, as I am on the subject, just two things I mention - first, that very morning I received an anonymous postcard. Although it was complete rubbish, it was the very first one I had ever received, and it niggled me a lot. What other things were being said about me? And the second was when Howard Wigginton, then chairman of the Young Conservatives, whispered to me just before I was due 'on' for my big moment, that a telegram had been received from the Leader, Edward Heath no less, wishing Chris the best of luck. As all four candidates were committed to his leadership, I remember thinking at the time it was a singularly inept thing to do - but the sending of the telegram to where the selection meeting was taking place with the likelihood that knowledge of it would 'get around', unsettled me still further at that time. In any event, it is ancient history now, and of course Chris was brilliant from all accounts.

But to return to Edward du Cann: I had known him slightly since I was Chairman of the Chichester Division and Leader of the Majority Group of the West Sussex County Council and he was presiding at one of the Party functions (as Chairman of the Party). This meant he stood receiving small fry such as myself to the line-up of VIPs, and when it came to my turn, he said, "and this is Barry Rose who should have got the Chichester seat". It was shortly after my own débâcle and at that time was feeling a bit low; one tends to remember things like that.

However, that aside I admire him for a number of reasons - first and foremost, one of his first posts was as clerk to a parish council (and a West Sussex one, to boot) at a time when the salary would have been minimal, if anything at all. But that aside it seemed to me he was the only member of the Cabinet who really understood what local government was all about at a time when Mr. Heath and Mr. Walker were doing their best to destroy it. Additionally, his performances on the B.B.C. "Any Questions" always struck me as wholly delightful, with his common-sense attitudes and when necessary his adoption of a broad Somerset accent mimicking his more rural constituents to introduce humour into the programme (I can never understand why he was dropped unless it is the traditional pro-Left bias of that otherwise mostly admirable institution).

Of course, subsequently he had his own problems and vanished from sight and sound - as a colleague of Tiny Rowland - who, alas, died all too soon bearing in mind what happened over Harrods. But while as Chairman of the Party he laid it down that not only would all the Conservative leaders of the county councils and county boroughs be invited to a quarterly meeting at Central Office, but also, if we had a particular matter we wished to discuss with any Minister, the Minister would in fact see us - obviously it was not a privilege to be exercised lightly.

Well, comprehensive education was such a subject - West Sussex was, I believe, one of the very first counties in the country to espouse the principle of comprehensive education (probably because many of its members were themselves products of public schools and comprehensive education seemed closest in theory to them) - but of course it is not, and has never been regarded as, a panacea for every educational situation: the great danger is when enthusiasm for it over-rides the common sense. As it happened, in my own council, I thought such a situation arose in one village. However, by un-fortunate chance I had an engagement at Blenheim Palace which conflicted with a meeting at County Hall - my wife and myself were to be presented to Queen Elizabeth the Queen Mother; in the event, we did not get there at all - the traffic was so appalling (despite having a professional driver) we had to miss Blenheim out entirely. Thus, to my shame, I missed the county council meeting and in my absence the scheme to 'go comprehensive' for that particular village was decided to be proceeded with - although on the surface, it looked typical of the botched-up schemes which were so common elsewhere in the country. And by the merest majority - whereas had I been present perhaps a referral to the Ministry of Education with a resultant in-quiry would have been decided upon - anyway, that was my belief.

Thus, I decided to exercise my option, as propounded by Edward du Cann, and asked to see the Secretary of State for

Education. I always prefer meetings on *my* home ground, so, instead of seeing her at the D. of E., I therefore invited the Secretary of State, who as it happened, was Mrs. Margaret Thatcher (as she then was) to luncheon at the Oxford and Cambridge University Club. She was to meet me at (I believe) 12.30 or 12.45 p.m. - but during the morning my wife telephoned to say that the Cabinet Office had been in touch, to say that because of a long Cabinet the Secretary of State would be 30 minutes late. In those days, ladies were entertained in a separate wing at the Club, and there was a writing desk situated (unseen from the entrance) immediately behind the porter's desk in the entrance hall which, when waiting for people, I often used; I told the porter I was expecting Mrs. Margaret Thatcher and he was to bring her to me the moment she arrived. I settled down to writing letters, and the next I heard was the voice which we were all to become familiar in later years, *"Who* does Mr. Barry Rose think he is?" in ringing tones. I rushed from my writing desk, and there was the porter rather as I imagine a rabbit must look, when confronted by a ferret, standing as if turned into stone.

Anyway, that was soon disposed of and we went up for luncheon: she looked so cool, so elegant and so beautiful. It was a good luncheon - I know we drank two bottles of wine, quite apart from what would have gone before, and I remember her very first remark: "Take out your diary, Mr. Rose, and write my personal address." Seeing my puzzlement, she said, "Don't you understand - you write to me at the Ministry or the House, and my officials will open the letter. At this very moment I expect your officials and my officials are discussing what we are discussing and seeing how they can stop us."

The rest of the conversation I remember equally clearly, which included (as I was supposed to be something of an authority on local government) a request from her for a book on the central and local government relationship. John Griffiths of the L.S.E. and himself a former councillor, had written in my opinion the best and indeed, at that time, the only work on the subject (although the author of two, but it might have been three *Labour* General Election Manifestos) his book nevertheless showed an accurate awareness of the subject - and someone like Mrs. Thatcher had the political *nous* to take the party-political aspect of his book for granted, before discounting it. Anyway, she took out a notebook, and said she would get a copy from the librarian. All in all, a delightful person - that Heath could have selected her as his "statutory woman" in his Cabinet, if anything, put him up several notches in my estimation. And then, at 3 p.m., her ministerial car arrived, and that was that. It would be an understatement and almost an insult to say of someone like her (now a world figure, of the top class) that I was most impressed. For what it is worth, I have held the opinion that the country was so disgusted by the *way* in which she was effectively dumped, and by such political pygmies, that the Conservatives will not return to power until the Conservative Party is forgiven for 'dumping' her in the way it did.

I later became the publisher for the Centre for Policy Studies - of which Mrs. Thatcher was President (aided of course by Keith Joseph who was regarded as the founder). Obviously, she knew that there was no possible profit in such a venture for me, and she wrote me a very appreciative letter of thanks for such help as we had been able to give the Centre - which was being run - as brilliantly as one would expect - by Alfred Sherman (*q.v.*) as Director.

At that stage, he was a particular friend of mine, and one evening we were having dinner (at Simpson's) and the conversation turned to the leadership of Edward Heath. Disquiet was everywhere, at least in the South East, where I was pretty closely in touch. Who was to be his successor? We went over various names in the Shadow Cabinet - the two of us were agreed on the names one or other of us brought up, and dismissed I am afraid rather contemptuously, and then Alfred said, "What about Margaret Thatcher?" I immediately dismissed this idea, with "But she's a woman." And then I thought back to that luncheon some years previously. By the end of that dinner, Margaret Thatcher was our joint choice.

I have little doubt that Alfred over-estimated my own importance in the Party (if I may say so, it was something I never did) but I *was* at that time holder of various offices in the South East, and I suppose it could have *looked* impressive - all I do know is that Alfred was at that time very knowledgeable and seemed on good terms with many of those on the 'right' of the Party, of which I was an insignificant member.

Now Alfred is generally credited with having been responsible for Margaret Thatcher having been chosen as Leader - personally, I believe that. And I would like to think that our dinner at Simpson's set light to the process that later resulted in her election as Leader.

* * * * *

A friend of mine - a doctor (A.S. Burne) who used to practise in the Pagham/Aldwick area, but it must be said, not very enthusiastically, as in effect he had retired when the Chinese Communists were in the process of taking over China and also the coal mine (owned by Westerners) of which he had been the medic. He duly came back to England.

As you entered his house, there was a large glittering sword standing in the hall. He told me it was a momento of the village in

China which he had left. Apparently, if an elderly person felt that life was becoming burdensome, he would ask to be executed - with a display of fireworks as his head was chopped off. It always took place on a Saturday afternoon - when the village went *en fete*. Come to think of it - not a bad way to go.

* * * * *

There was a proposal to build an atomic power station at Earnley, in the Manhood of Selsey, and Walter 'Bill' Loveys, the M.P. for Chichester, accompanied one of the Manhood's farmers to see the Minister who would be responsible if the decision went ahead. The farmer and the Minister and the M.P. had a reasonably rational discussion and then the farmer, without warning, brought to the ministerial table his attaché case, opened it, and emptied out the contents - the rich soil of the parish of Earnley "That's the sort of good agricultural land you'll be losing if this goes through," he said. Bill thought of the glistening Ministerial table as it had been and the earth suddenly plonked upon it by *his* constituent - the Minister was evidently impressed, for no atomic power station was ever built there. In the ultimate sense, direct action - a very effective act of political persuasion.

The man who was the leader of the campaign against the atomic power station was a local solicitor, Norman Hignett, partner in a local firm of great respectability, and Her Majesty's Coroner for Chichester, no less. I knew him quite well - he had formerly been at Butterworths - and at meetings (and in court) he was a really able and distinguished advocate. As chairman of the campaign, I have little doubt he made many new clients both for himself and his firm, but soon the city of Chichester was awash with rumour. Both his spending and his sex life caused more than the odd eyebrow to be raised in professional circles - and also in non-professional ones (because of my friendship with Marjorie Acford, the then editor of the *Chichester Observer* and repository of all gossip, I was kept well posted).

One story delighted me enormously - Tangmere was a fighter base during the Battle of Britain, and the cocktail bar of a certain Chichester public house (no longer in existence) was the Officers' Mess. Remember that during the War beer (like everything else) was in short supply - but because of Tangmere's importance in terms of defence, and an understanding of the pressures and strains of the men fighting in the Battle of Britain - whoever else went short of beer, *that* public house did not. The landlord, a man of gargantuan dimensions, very naturally stood to profit vastly from this - but the Government in 1939 (remembering the vast profiteering of the First World War) had wisely put a clamp upon excess profits; the landlord was not going to be beaten by a thing like that, and he had a suitcase, which no doubt he placed each night under his bed (perhaps the suitcase is apocryphal). He also had an acute business sense: the members of the Mess were invited to put £1 in the kitty, "and drink as much beer as you like." It requires no financial genius to understand that three or four young men forming a 'school' would together have had some difficulty in consuming say, 15 pints between them which with beer at less than a shilling a pint left a very substantial margin of profit from the £1 given at the beginning of the session. More for that suitcase, from men who perhaps next day would lose their lives or be terribly burnt and disfigured. [Warning! I was not a member of the Officers' Mess; what I say is hearsay only - and in fairness, I do know that the publican's wife - whose place in her husband's life was taken over by one of his barmaids, worked so hard for service charities.]

And then enter Mr. Hignett - eminent local solicitor, partner of old-established firm - who was able to whisper that he could invest the contents of the suitcase about which the Government must never know anything and confidentiality was the name of the game. The suitcase was handed over, and no doubt Mr. Hignett was able to put it to a good use. Good use - ah, yes. On one occasion, a friend of mine, Richard ("Dickie") Austin, a jeweller by trade, but incidentally a War-time navigator who wrote a book which I published, received a telephone call - could he arrange for a couple of trays of "goodies" to be taken to Mr. Hignett's establishment in Birdham (a village on the outskirts of Chichester). His partner went with the trays of "goodies" to find Mr. Hignett in bed with two young ladies indecorously clad. He asked each of the young ladies to take what took their fancy, and the trays of rings thus depleted were returned to the jewellers in Chichester. So you will see therefore that the publican's money was indeed put to a good use.

But more seriously, the good as well as the bad who were defrauded were numerous - it was said at that time to be one of the most serious defalcations by a solicitor, ever, in this country - and the Police had only a rudimentary idea of the total involved - who, for example, like the publican - could not make a complaint; who also, like the purely respectable but socially prominent, could admit to a relationship with Hignett? Or admit to having hidden from the tax man money if not illegally made, then certainly illegally not disclosed. Far better to swallow hard and forget all about it. The City of Chichester had never experienced anything like it before, but in due course he was arrested and put on bail. He duly jumped bail, and went to France, but ran out of money, and rather foolishly flew back to England to get some more. He was picked up and his bail was not renewed. The Clerk to the Magistrates (Bill Booker) phoned me to say that Hignett would be appearing in court later that day, and as such occasions were rare, perhaps I would like to come as a spectator. The bail was estreated (I think it was £8,000, and I knew one of the chaps who had to shell out: he told me Hignett had telephoned him to say he was coming back; he was sore because he had telephoned the Police who had picked Hignett up, but who otherwise would not have known he was back in England - even so, the bail was still estreated).

Hignett was sentenced to either six or seven years (I forget which) and on his release, he wrote a book called *Portrait in Grey*. It was the most powerful argument for penological reform (and I had read many on the subject) I had seen, but I said to my friends at the time - that bearing in mind the unflattering way in which prison officers were depicted - he could never go back to prison. Soon after his release, he was arrested for fraud, and later, was duly fished out of a London canal before his trial. A coroner's inquest made a finding of suicide.

* * * * *

I was invited to the Bowmakers' dinner - a livery company which had the belief that if King Charles's army had depended upon bow and arrow, they would have won the Civil War - instead of that, they relied upon the slow-loading, high self-injury inflicting, newly invented flintlocks. That year's Master was Bill Williams (*q.v.*) and it so happened that the dinner was a few months after the *Lady Chatterley* obscenity case - and Bill's cousin, Sir Allen Lane, the founder of *Penguin Books* and its publisher, was on my left, and on my right (Mr. Mervyn Griffith-Jones who prosecuted at the trial, who alas, will always be remembered for his observations to the jury, that they had to ask themselves whether this was the sort of book they would wish their maidservants to read, and in consequence, was reduced almost to a figure of fun by the national media). It was the first time the two had seen each other since the trial and, of course, as might be expected, both were civil and indeed friendly, towards each other.

It was a ridiculous trial - leading prelates and academics going into the witness box to say what a wonderful piece of literature it was, whereas in my opinion it was truly just rubbish with Lawrence using naughty words to get them out of his system. Personally I found the book boring almost to the point of disbelief. Later, a friend at the DPP's office asked me if I had any suggestions as to whom they could get as witnesses on any such future occasion or whom to consult as to whether to prosecute at all. I am a Member of the Royal Society of Literature, and I suggested that the Society in future be asked to nominate someone. I do not know if the suggestion was followed up, but the procession of worthy people to praise Lady Chatterley did, I am sure, far more harm than good - regardless of its alleged literary qualities.

* * * * *

Sir Frank Layfield was, I suppose, just a few years younger than Bill Williams (*q.v.*) and Sir Desmond Heap (*q.v.*) and therefore had the greater all-round knowledge of local government of anyone I knew at that period. I always felt rather sorry for Layfield - his sense of public duty had tied him down to such mega-inquiries as Sizewell B, Local Government Finance and Terminal Five. He was such a nice chap - I don't think he had an idea who I was, but we used to chat from time to time (we were both members of the same clubs) - a few months before his death, we talked of the mess in which local government found itself. He said that looking back, he supposed the 1933 Local Government Act came closest to perfection of all the Local Government Acts he had known.

If I may digress for a moment - it seems that I spent a significant part of my local government life (a cumulative period of 34 years on the various local authorities) engaged in defending myself in respect of threatened libel/slander actions. Rarely have things seemed to work out as I planned. I had been a member of the Chichester R.D.C. for about nine years, and had been Chairman of its major spending committees for about five of those years; I then was very briefly chairman of its planning committee of the R.D.C. Normally, we held our meetings in the council chamber (a rather grand name for what was a quite ordinary, non-purpose built room), and the chairman of the committee sat on a chair with his/her officials on either side on a dias, while the committee clerks sat at a table below.

I was unhappy (and I had my reasons) with the impartiality of the advice given the committee in relation to "my" parish and I planned to resign the chairmanship after reading the statement I had prepared, and in a dignified manner, walk out. Nothing more. But alas, the council chamber was being used by the district auditor, and instead, with no advance warning, we were transferred to hold the meeting in the much smaller, engineer and surveyor's room, where we were jammed so tightly together that literally I could not get out without "Excuse me, Sir", every few inches. I think it is fair to say that the meeting had been stunned, metaphorically, by what I said, and as a result of time taken by me to get out, they recovered and one member jumped up and said, "We're not going to let Barry Rose go like this" and proposed a vote of confidence which was carried while I was still struggling to get out.

I knew, as every local authority member knew (or did know before party politics took over) that an individual member does not stand a chance - he fights on his own, whereas in such cases the officers very naturally have the support of one or other of the professional associations - but I did not want to fight at all - just say what I had to say, resign from the chairmanship, and to go quietly (no press were present and the minutes would merely have recorded the fact of my resignation and the vice-chairman taking my place). But the well-meant vote of confidence altered everything. As it was, the following week I was almost torn apart when the counter-attack took place; the minutes of *this* meeting, to say the very least, were as well as the earlier ones, very hostile to me, so I had to retaliate in the terms permitted under the council's standing orders. As a result I was threatened with libel (*sic*) proceedings after I had distributed what I said at that council meeting (open to the press, whereas at that time committee meetings were not so open). I was then threatened by the county council arising from a letter which they had seen on the Chichester R.D.C. file. I was threatened with all sorts of things, and I confess to being relieved I was not married at that time, because my wife would have been not best pleased by the fusillade of threats made against me - as of course later was the case with the Clerk of the Bognor Regis U.D.C. Looking back, if the district auditor had not wanted our usual council meeting room and I could have slipped out after my resignation speech - it would all have passed over peacefully; as it was, I lost a good friend of many years standing - the learned clerk (a barrister) who for some reason thought I was attacking *him*. He counter-attacked on that assumption. I lost (well, actually we both lost, as no one can be a winner in a situation like this) the pitched battle that took place between us (obviously I knew who I had in mind when I made my original resignation speech as I suspect did two other senior chief officers who remained friendly towards me throughout) but once I was being threatened with libel proceedings, I had to 'clam up' - he, poor chap, died before peace could be re-established between us. But one good thing came out of it all - I met Arnold Goodman [subsequently Lord Goodman] who acted for me, and who advised me most effectively on each step. He was invaluable then, and subsequently one of his partners, with the then Clerk of the Bognor Regis U.D.C. some time later.

In retrospect, I wish I had never said anything at all but instead spoken privately to the Clerk - however, one can never job backwards, and in any event, we had just taken over the *Police Journal*, and I had to give up the council in any event as a result of extra pressure of work in my office; also, I had just moved into Bognor.

* * * * *

Noel Williamson (*q.v.*), was invited to stay for a weekend at Craigweil House, near Bognor. This was in 1917 or 1918 and he would have been on leave from the Western Front - he recalled his stay particularly because - according to him - there was just one bathroom for the 18 house guests; they were also entertained by the host's mistress not his wife. At the end of the world war, the House was extended and virtually rebuilt, so we may expect that by the time King George V had been sent there by his physicians to recuperate after a lung infection, the House would have been a little more comfortable. I well remember as a small boy taken to the outposts of the House and being awed by the sentries on duty on the shingle.

But certainly, Bognor was never the same again - to start with, a group of traders petitioned the Privy Council to have "Regis" incorporated into its name, which was agreed. Why this should have been so I have never been able to understand, for the King never stayed in Bognor - he stayed in Craigweil, which was then a part of the Parish of Pagham next door. (The West Sussex county council made an Order in 1934 under the 1933 Local Government

Act saying that henceforth Craigweil was to be part of Bognor Regis - but at the time the King stayed in the area in 1928-9, it was still Pagham.) Oddly, some of the older institutions such as the Church will have nothing to do with the Regis and anyway, many seem to call it Butlin Regis these days.

However, to continue - the King returned in due course to Buckingham Palace, and Sir Arthur du Crow, the owner of Craigweil House, sent him a bill for the occupation of the house. One can imagine that this would have almost resulted in a relapse, for whoever heard of the King (*any* King) being charged for having bestowed the honour of his company, but the bill was paid, and in due course Sir Arthur duly demolished the House and on its site and surrounding grounds, created a small housing estate (where for some years I lived myself). I noticed his name never seemed to figure in the Honours Lists.

The contents of the House found their way in various directions - the builders of the hotel used by me to entertain Mr. Farey-Jones (*q.v.*) actually bought the King's bath, which again might not have been pleasing to the Royal Majesty. A few years later, in 1936, the King again fell ill; again his physicians advised him to go to Bognor, but this time, summoning up whatever reserves of strength he had left, he is said to have delivered himself, before expiring, of the immortal phrase, "Bugger Bognor".

Had this remark remained confined to the Royal sickroom, perhaps no harm would have been done - but the phrase escaped so that today, if one is foolish enough to admit one's home is in that resort, it is invariably followed by "Oh yes - bugger Bognor, isn't it?" followed by peals of laughter as if the person concerned has delivered himself of some great witticism.

To those who are patient enough to listen, I tell them that *if* King George did say this (and Kenneth Rose, author of the

111

definitive work on the King, seems to be in little doubt as to the provenance of it) then one must remember that George V was known as the Sailor King - and according to Dr. Johnson's *Dictionary*, bugger is a term of affection used between sailors - *ergo*, he was really quite fond of the place. [Although I notice that Dr. Bowdler or one of his persuasion has expunged that particular definition from the 2nd edition. And when I wrote to the *Bognor Regis Observer* pointing out my likely explanation, the editor duly expunged the reference to bugger - thus, in Bognor at any rate, the spirit of Dr. Bowdler lives on.]

* * * * *

The Press Club was a place I found extraordinarily useful. It was centred within yards of Dr Samuel Johnson's House, at the back of Fleet Street, and although non-residential, it had an excellent restaurant run by a man called Soloman, who once said to me that the Club seemed to think he was making a fortune out of the concession: he promised me he was not. (The restaurant served luncheon, not dinner.) It was convenient for me especially, since it was close to the Temple on one side, Lincoln's Inn and Gray's Inn not too far away on the other. The Club had no rules about business matters being discussed; therefore my guests and I would talk about the commissioning of a book or article, or whatever, we would have a drink and they would go back to their chambers or, all business matters out of the way, have dinner with me somewhere else. It was also useful to know that the bar remained open until 2 a.m., so that if the worst came to the worst, and I missed my last train, there was a milk and newspaper train, stopping at every station (so one did not do it often).

Then Mr Soloman departed, and the Club Secretary took over the responsibility of the restaurant in addition to the administration of the Club generally. Did I hear someone say something about a cobbler and his last?

Thus one day. I checked in, although strangely, there was no one to take one's hat, and started climbing the stairs to the bar - where there was a pleasing assortment of cartoons of people famous (or infamous) in the press world on the wall, lining the stairs. Or rather, I should say, had been. Now the walls were bare. I reached the top of the stairs and saw men putting chairs on tables, etc. The bar was closed; of the barman there was no sign. It is no exaggeration to say that I actually stumbled backwards down some of the stairs in shock. By this time, the hat-check girl was back on duty: "Isn't it terrible, Mr Rose. The brokers' men."

And thus the Press Club [that edition] was no more.

* * * * *

Bognor Regis was such a pleasant town - virtually no crime, and with a range of good shops; it was (as of course it still is) in the middle of the flattest part of England, the coastal fringe between Worthing and the Manhood of Selsey, which was why heart specialists recommended their patients to live there; it had three live theatres during the "season", and three cinemas. Today, we have a holiday camp which used to be called Butlins, but which is now called something else, plus two (not one, but *two*) tattooists; one council-owned theatre has long been replaced by a concrete area to enable (mostly) the young to test their skills with skateboards and there is actually a train travelling the length of the promenade during the summer months and a theatre also owned by the council but whose future seems somewhat precarious, and one cinema outside Butlins. O joy unconfined. I can call to mind two very good shops closed as a result of petty thieving; others have had to depart the world's scene as a result of the arrival of the multiples. Bognor indeed is not what it was, and doubtless there are those who say it is far better than it was, but I suppose the most significant reason for the change in the history of the town since the arrival of Mr. Hotham in the 17th century, was the arrival of Mr. Butlin in the 20th - even although the latter's effect did not reach its full potential until after the War. All the fun of the fair was indeed provided by Mr. Butlin (as he then was) on the front just east of the Pier - and to be frank, to some eyes, a small area did look a bit of a mess. The leases had some distance to run, so a deal was set up - that Butlins would leave their position on the front with its shooting gallery, dodgem-cars, etc., and head east, to a village (Felpham) absorbed into Bognor by County Council diktat in 1934. In Felpham there was an area consisting of marshland which (I was told) had some unique specimens of wildlife, about which a Mr. Venables would write enthusiastically in his local newspaper column. There, said Mr. Butlin, we would like to build a holiday camp - instead of being a wasteland of marsh (as he called it). Intelligent enough to anticipate gasps of horror, it was explained that the old fairground image of Butlins was no longer applicable to his holiday camps - he suggested that some people in positions of power and authority in Bognor and in the Planning Authority (West Sussex County Council) should visit one of his exciting new holiday camps and see for themselves? A few days in North Wales would show them what a modern Butlin camp was like, not to be feared, but to be welcomed.

According to my informant Jim Earle (a former sergeant in the Metropolitan Police and then a licensee in Bognor, having just retired from the chair of the Bognor Regis U.D.C.) he and a few of his particular buddies on the Council had gone together in the absence on holiday of the then Clerk to the Council (Mr. R.W.J. Hill), to his office, and had found this suggestion from Mr. Butlin and decided to activate it. (But I don't suppose it was quite like that! Nothing ever is!)

All this was as a prelude to the announcement which arrived like a thunderclap - the very first that the people of Bognor and Felpham knew of the proposal in the town was *after* planning consent for the holiday camp had been given with a 100-year lease on the land at Felpham - whose residents were mostly affected, not being consulted at all. Naturally, all hell broke loose.

Mrs. Thatcher (as she then was) introduced her Private Member's Bill for the Admission of the Press to Local Authority Committee Meetings. There was also myself (says he modestly) for once ahead of the crowd, speaking on the same subject to various national platforms and at the Rural District Councils Association at Llandudno, when I was followed by the so-formidable Dame Evelyn Sharp, who was to praise my contribution. So there! What I am trying to say is that "secrecy" in local government was on its way out.

I digress. Of course Bognor has one of the most unattractive place names of any town in the U.K. - any town that *I* can think of, anyway. Yet undeniably it has a soft climate, is absolutely flat, and was probably the first real seaside resort in the country - Brighton was to come later - Richard Hotham invested his own fortune from profits made from the South Seas Bubble and tried to alter things by calling it Hothampton. But the residents, after taking his money, rejected his name, and the town went back to being Bognor after his death.

Now seaside towns seem to attract a 'flashy' type of reputation - I suppose it is partly because they have to live somewhat precariously during the 'season' - that short period of the year when hotels and boarding houses and restaurants and places of recreation must somehow make sufficient money to survive for the remaining 7 or 8 months of the year.

These days, we hear a lot about corruption in public life and at Westminster - with allegations of sleaze and other misbehaviour - yet in my own lifetime there has only been one instance that I can recall of actual corruption in Government and it concerned a junior Minister in the Attlee Administration in the post-war Labour Government. There it concerned the grant of a building licence for the Royal Norfolk Hotel in Bognor - an hotel in a wonderful situation facing the sea. It had been occupied by troops during the war, and in order to give priority to home building and rebuilding, licences had to be obtained for anything like the repair of an hotel - a Mr. Stanley bribed the junior Minister with a suit of clothes for the licence; poor fellow, he (the Minister) was sent to prison whilst Mr. Stanley somewhat hurriedly, left these shores and went to Israel.

I mention this as indicating the sort of culture which *can* exist in a decent town. Mr. Henry Brooke, former Conservative Leader of the London County Council (in other words, someone who would have known a little about local government) and when he paid a visit to Bognor, it was as Minister of Housing and Local Government) he was importuned by councillors to help the 'clear up' of the town by the making of an order defining an area of comprehensive redevelopment. The Minister gave an undertaking to this effect - and let us face it - part of Bognor on its front east of the Pier *did* look in need of comprehensive renewal - but to compare Bognor because it had a few tatty amusements arcades, etc. with towns such as Plymouth and Portsmouth and the Northern industrial cities which had suffered terribly from bombing during the war, which were intended to be the main beneficiaries of the planning policy of comprehensive area redevelopment, was plainly ridiculous. It meant that instead of allowing gradual redevelopment to take place, it effectively sterilized *all* redevelopment which was put on hold for many years for a significant swathe of the town because, in the order of priorities, West Sussex County Council, as the planning authority, had many other priorities - Gatwick and the New Town of Crawley were naturally in the forefront of the county's scheme of things, and were much more important than Bognor - except, of course, to the residents of Bognor.

And almost by some miracle, the small area of the 'tatty bits' which were to go as this result of the 'bargain' made over the creation of Butlins, still remained. After all, who on earth would wish to occupy premises or build new ones which might be demolished any day when the redevelopment started? Apart from Crawley, so far as I can recollect, there was no party political control of any council in West Sussex, apart from individual members, other elected members were all independent, so there was no cutting edge given by elected members.

Therefore, one day I was reading a newspaper at luncheon and read to my astonishment that Bognor Regis the previous night had granted Butlin permission to build a holiday camp at Felpham (*q.v.*). In common with the rest of Bognor, I was stunned. Later, I was to hear part of the inside story from the area planning officer - how he and other officials, and members and officials of the Bognor Regis U.D.C. had gone to a Butlin Camp in Wales for a weekend, in conditions of some secrecy, in order that they might be reassured that the type of camp envisaged bore no relation to the type of camp dating back to pre-war days.

Of course, in the town itself some said it was a marvellous opportunity for the town, and another faction said the opposite - but permission had already been given anyway and that was that. It was my belief (which of course I cannot substantiate) that the subsequent Skeffington Report (which brought into existence the requirements of the planning authority to advertise each planning application) came about partially as a result of what happened in Bognor over Butlins.

Years and years later, two councillors from the Bognor Regis U.D.C., who had been deeply involved in the earlier matter at Bognor, who were also members of the West Sussex County Council, gave evidence at a public inquiry at Minehead in Somerset, where Butlins had made application for a holiday camp there, extolling the camp at Bognor Regis and saying the citizens of Bognor to this [that] day were well pleased with that decision. They must have been much dismayed when their words were reported in the *Daily Telegraph*, so that Bognor Regis could *read* what had been said in the report of the proceedings at Minehead and ascribing such views to them. It would be difficult to find a significant number of the citizens of Bognor in favour of the camp at any time since its arrival in the town, although to be fair, I hear it has improved considerably since earlier days and later, when it was so soundly criticized by the B.B.C. Radio Holidays programme - but that of course is of benefit to holiday-makers - not much value in it for residents. But let us be optimistic about its future.

* * * * *

Dr. Michael Ayres was appointed Medical Officer of Health (when there were such creatures) for Bognor Regis U.D.C. (when there was such a body) and also Assistant (or it might have been Deputy) M.O.H. for West Sussex county council, in 1922 or 1923. He and I found ourselves on the same committee of the county council when he retired, and we gravitated towards each other. He told me that when he was newly appointed to the county council, they were carrying out some sort of inquiry into the reasons for the high incidence of incest in certain areas. The census ultimately centred upon a wholly delightful village lying between Chichester (then as now the county town) and Midhurst, a small town, at the crest of the Downs to the North. The conclusion was drawn from the report that situated as it was between two towns, with steep hills on either side, the young men of the village found the physical effort of going downhill to Chichester and returning uphill, and for Midhurst, exactly the reverse, excessive. Therefore, an unhealthy proportion stayed put in the village for their sexual pleasure with the inevitable result. Of course, in those days, cars were a rarity, and probably bikes were not all that easy to come by on an agricultural worker's wage.

Michael was a fund of stories - as when M.O.H. for Bognor, he carried out an inspection of a small zoo, on the seafront, owned and operated by Billy Butlin (long before his knighthood). He found the conditions completely unacceptable, and gave Butlin one week to clean up the "zoo", with its solitary dispirited lion leading a small contingent of other animals, or be closed down. As soon as Butlin was persuaded that Michael Ayres meant business (i.e., was incorruptible) the work was done and a notice put up outside claiming, "As approved by Bognor's Medical Officer of Health." Michael of course demanded its immediate removal.

Butlin, I suppose, had yet to make his first million, and in the mid-thirties had thought of a device which he put to the then tenant farmer of Church Farm, Pagham (*q.v.*) - one John Wensley who was the farmer before Dutton (*q.v.*) or Hender (*q.v.*). or perhaps it was a joint enterprise, probably embarked upon over a drink. The story was put around that the lion had escaped, had killed sheep at Church Farm and was roaming the district frightening the locals. Well, who wouldn't be scared? The intrepid Police, however, did not shoot the lion, but arrested the farmer for his waste of police time and I suspect in relation to other charges as well. Ultimately, he was fined - I seem to remember it was £200 - with costs; Mr. Butlin, who had thought up the whole scheme as a publicity stunt for his zoo, was not charged at all. The national papers especially the tabloids like the *Mirror* and the *Sketch*, and also the *Mail*, had

119

made a huge fuss of the supposed escape. In publicity terms, it certainly paid off.

The years pass, and in the late forties Mr. Wensley, the farmer, was living in somewhat straitened circumstances; he wrote to Mr. Butlin explaining his new situation, and asking Butlin (by this time a millionaire) whether he would be good enough to refund the fine he had had to pay. I am sure you can guess the answer.

* * * * *

W.H.G. Cocks was county treasurer of Glamorgan. Most improbably, I should add, as normally Welsh councils liked to appoint one of their own kind, and Harry was English. But I would think their council's affairs had got into a bit of a mess - his predecessor for example, had known little or nothing about local government finance before joining the council - he had been employed in a Justices' Clerk's office - whereas Harry had come into Glamorgan from being borough treasurer of Dagenham borough council, as it was then. Dagenham was an East End of London borough, where the meetings in winter-time went on interminably. He told me the reason: the members found the council committee rooms warm, if they shortened the proceedings and went home their houses would be very cold. Thus, poverty before the War: and it also says something about the quality of local government. I think it was Herbert Morrison who said he would build the Tories out of London, and Dagenham would have been one of his first successes in this direction - aided, of course, by the arch-capitalist Henry Ford, who decided to build his immense factory there. When Dame Shirley Porter (then Leader of Westminster City Council) was accused of attempting the same thing on a much more modest scale in Westminster of building Labour out of that City, it was 50-60 years later and she was fined

£30 million (against which she appealed and won. However, subsequently there was an appeal against the appeal which succeeded, and Dame Shirley, as I write, is back in square one).

However, to return to Harry Cocks, who on retirement, lived in one half of the mansion previously owned by Lord Maugham, the former Lord Chancellor, brother of Somerset Maugham. He told me that the cheques he received from the *J.P.* had gone to help pay for his son's education; another contributor, A.C.L. Morrison, Chief Clerk at Bow Street Magistrates' court, when I visited him at his house in Maidenhead, took me outside to have a good view of it, and said that he had bought it with fees for his contributions for the *J.P.*; he did not believe in getting into debt, not even a mortgage, and put the money into a building society until he had enough to pay for his house outright. Harry later wrote for *Local Government Review* when I split it away from the *J.P.*, and made it a separate entity and became financial editor. It is nice to see people gaining some personal benefit from the journals, and not just writing for the love of it - after all did not Dr. Johnson, the great Dr. Johnson, say that no one but a blockhead wrote except for money? (As I was editor of *Rural District Review* for three or four years, literary editor of the *Chichester Observer* for two or three years, and wrote numerous articles for the Bognor and Chichester local press on environmental matters - none of which, alas! resulted in payment, I know a little myself about being a blockhead.) Both Cocks and Morrison got C.B.E.s, so their work did not go entirely unnoticed, although of course their awards had to do with their everyday tasks, and not for anything they did for the 'J.P.'.

As a corollary to that, I remember meeting a member of the judiciary whose article had appeared that day in the *Daily Telegraph* and congratulating him upon it. He volunteered the information the number of hundreds of pounds he had been paid for it - which I suspect he thought was too much - for he added "of course it knocks people like you right out of the market." Of course it does - a splendid journal selling at most to a few thousand people cannot possibly compete in terms of fees with a newspaper selling a million copies a day, with advertising revenue to match.

* * * * *

Chris Chataway's by-election for the Chichester constituency was under way, and Iain MacLeod and his wife, now Baroness MacLeod, came down to support him at two meetings. It was my press day, so although I could not get home in time for the small (early) dinner party that my wife gave in his honour and arrived just as they were about to leave, with the Central Office agent with them. However, he spoke at two meetings that early evening on opposite geographical sides of the constituency, and then returned for a party we were giving later in the evening. It was a punishing regime for a fit man - but he was in pain throughout, and when it was suggested he should not come to our party, but begin the journey back to London, he said simply "I promised the Barry Roses I'd be back for their party, and I am not going to disappoint them." He left at about 11.15 to begin his journey back to London; what a marvellous man.

In my early life, I used to read *The Economist, Time and Tide, Truth, John o'London's, New Statesman* and *Spectator* - as the years went by, they either closed down or I no longer had time to read them - except the *Spectator*, of which Iain MacLeod was then editor. Compared with today, it was a skimpy little thing, with a tiny circulation, and I think he was fascinated that he had found - in the wilds of Bognor Regis - someone who actually bought and read *his* journal. Of course, now it is a splendid journal - with probably seven or eight times the circulation, but editorially, it was also pretty good in his day.

Thanks to the Heath/Walker reforms otherwise called the destruction of local government (since then over-ridden by subsequent "reforms" - the corpse having been dug up and kicked around still further), there is now - no such thing as an alderman. These were creatures who were elected by councillors (generally from elected members) for six years at a time who were elected by the electorate for three years. Historically, they dated back to Saxon times, and therefore were ripe for abolition. (I suppose I have to come clean - and admit that for a very few weeks, I was an alderman myself - I believe I was the last one ever to be elected, and when the West Sussex County Council Mark One slid into history, I decided to go with it on the very same day and not stay for the final 12 months in the condemned cell, waiting for the current of the brand new local government to surge through the nation's veins). Aldermen had the advantage of keeping experienced members still on the council (and although West Sussex never, in my time, elected aldermen from outside the council, it could be used with great advantage to bring in people who were experienced in various fields but who were not and had never been, members of the council). (I tried to do it, once, with Col. Freddy Gough, the former M.P. for Horsham, who would have been a good chap to have on board the County Council - he suspected skullduggery in the count, as he was not - by the narrowest of margins, elected. I believe he would have contributed a lot to its work had it been otherwise. But he would, undoubtedly, have been unpopular with many members. As I was not present at the count, I will merely say many of the Conservative Group were like myself, unhappy at the result and the way the count had been conducted.)

Well, West Sussex was predominately Conservative during my time - I think I am right in saying that 79 out of 96 were Conservative (after some internal reorganisation of boundaries, etc.

it was reduced to 72 out of 84). It was still a very sizeable majority, but of course the aldermen represented one sixth of the number of members, and West Sussex, when it was under Independent control would only elect two Labour aldermen, which was proportionate to the number of Labour members. One of these was a gifted member called Dr. Ivan Clout - a doctor of medicine, and he came from Crawley. He was someone who was regarded as a member of the hard Left and was rather feared by all except the liberal-Left among the Conservatives. When he decided to stand down, therefore, one Labour Member would be "traded" for him as his replacement, and the Labour man (Bob May) selected was a very popular member (which I think I can fairly say Dr. Clout was not - respected certainly, but liked, never, except possibly, by some of the far-Left on the Conservative side). It was my job to propose to the meeting that his replacement should be made. On my brief walk from my office to County Hall, I thought of what to say, "Never cast a May till a Clout be out." It went down well.

* * * * *

One of the most remarkable men I ever met was the Reverend Dr. W.J. Bolt, LL.M. He had been Vicar of the improbably named parish of Sheepwash in Devon, but he had answered the call of the Metropolis, and went to the London School of Economics to read for a Ph.D. in criminology - his examiner being the distinguished criminologist (and former Judge from Berlin) Hermann Mannheim. Mannheim (a delightful man, who was a refugee from Hitler) gave Bolt the task of writing a thesis on the influence of the *Justice of the Peace* in the development of criminology in the first 100 years of its existence (1837-1936). Naturally, having left his living in

Sheepwash, he had to accept in substitution one of the poorest parishes of Inner London. I am quite sure he was a good and holy man; having got his PhD, he wrote extensively for the *J.P.* initially from his reading of its history, and in due course, wrote asking me whether he could visit "the shrine" (his description). My office at that time was situated immediately opposite the since transformed public house *The Prince Arthur*, in Little London, Chichester, and I had an unworthy suspicion that he had called in there on his way to see me. I offered modest hospitality in my own office, and by my [then] standards at least, we had very little to drink before we set sail for *The Ship Hotel* in North Street, for luncheon. There, was to be seen Peter May, one of my cricketing heroes, also engaged upon luncheon (he was the guest of a sports shop in South Street, which he had opened earlier that morning).

The behaviour of Dr. Bolt was, to say the least, erratic, and Peter May could hardly take his eyes off him, especially when he unzipped himself as he was about to enter the still-room of the hotel in the erroneous belief it was the men's room; there, he was steered diplomatically in the right direction. Some minutes later, hearing an altercation, I went into the hall of the hotel to find Bolt trying to mount the stairs leading to the residential part of the hotel, declaiming, as the head waiter held him at bay on the stairs, that he (the waiter) was attempting to prevent him seeing his friend Mr. Rose.

However, all was forgiven, for Bolt wrote like an angel, and in due course even Emery (my managing director) noticed his contributions. "Rose, I would like to meet this Dr. Bolt." "He's not really your cup of tea." "Allow me to be the best judge of that," came the somewhat frosty response, and I was left to arrange details for us to meet at the Waldorf, where Emery seemed to have a permanent table.

I think it would be fair to say that the luncheon was not an outstanding success: Bolt was, to start with, about 30 minutes late; after formal introductions had been effected, he was asked what he would like for an aperitif. Emery was a dry sherry man; I fancy I followed suit, and Bolt opted for a pint of bitter. That out of the way, he asked Emery - Mr. Eemery - (a pronunciation he stuck to and which did not please, for the rest of the luncheon) what he did. "I am Managing Director of Butterworths," said Emery, with just a little pride. "Oh yes," said Bolt, "they're small text-book publishers, aren't they?" "If you regard *Halsbury's Laws of England, The British and Empire Digest, Lumley's Public Health Acts* as small textbooks, yes, I suppose we are," replied Emery, plainly nettled. [For the uninitiated, such works are multi-volumed, and seem about the length of the *Encyclopaedia Britannica*.]

With our first course, "What would you like, Dr. Bolt?" "Potted shrimps," [or whatever it was] "and a pint of bitter." For the entrée, "What would you like, Dr. Bolt?" "A fillet steak," said Bolt, "and a pint of bitter." Half way through that course, he asked for and received a further pint of bitter. And for a finale, it was "Tapioca pudding, and a pint of bitter". Emery left to return to Butterworths with a somewhat thin-lipped injunction to me to look after Bolt for the remainder of the luncheon.

I never recall Emery asking to meet another contributor to the *J.P.*. As for Bolt, he continued writing for the *J.P.* for many years; as I have said, he wrote like an angel. I have mentioned some of his eccentricities: however, he was a good man - in addition to his ecclesiastical and other duties, he was an expert on company law, and advised a number of city firms, and was active as a Conservative: indeed, on the eve of his addressing one annual conference at Brighton, (where it will be appreciated that it was a rare sight for someone wearing a dog collar to speak "party politically" in the Conservative cause - it so happened, on housing problems in the inner cities), he asked me to call for him at his hotel on the way to the Reception in the Dome. It was a mistake on my part to have agreed. At the time, I had a girl-friend in Brighton, and when we called to pick him up to attend the reception where, with the other 3,500-odd delegates, we were to have our hands shaken by Mr. R.A. Butler, no less, we found ourselves spending most of the time walking him round one of the Brighton squares to enable him to be in a fit state to shake that hand. It was certainly not the way I had hoped we would be spending the evening. As for Bolt, he ultimately retired to Ely, just outside Cardiff, where he became an advocate for the temperance movement.

* * * * *

Betty Hand and her husband Bill used to run a pub in Chichester called the *Hole in the Wall*. She was an extraordinarily talented woman: at one stage (until her position as - in my opinion - premier chef in the city was challenged by someone who had been chef at the *Le Caprice* and *The Ivy*, in due course brought a new standard of cuisine to Chichester) her establishment was a very popular eating house in the city; her husband Bill was a genial host and very knowledgeable about wine. I mention Betty now since of all the people I have known over the years, she was the most truly wedded to racial and religious harmony. Born in the East End of London, at a time when racial tension against the Jews was at its height, she told me that at school, for religious worship, she would go where-ever she pleased of all the religious denominations "on offer" to be with a current friend; racially, when Sir Oswald Mosley agitated in the heart of the East End against the Jews, she witnessed many terrible instances of brutality by "Blackshirts" (the uniform used by men and women of the Union of Fascists in imitation of their Italian and German prototypes). The uniforms were banned by Stanley Baldwin's Conservative Government, and the first prosecution under the Act making the wearing of such uniforms illegal was undertaken against Mosley by Desmond Heap (*q.v.*) - at that time in his career the prosecuting solicitor for Leeds Corporation.

Then the War and the bombs came; she, like many others, was made homeless, and who should she see also made homeless, as they queued for food and blankets - but one of the Blackshirts of pre-War years. She made some cutting observation to him, and he apparently replied rather along these lines: "Mosley offered me trousers when my arse was sticking out and a shirt and boots. No one else offered me anything." To think that political faith can be founded upon such a basic want as a pair of trousers!

* * * * *

One of my friends, Noel Williamson (*q.v.*), found himself at a dinner party given by Sir Oswald Mosley (or presumably, his wife) before the War. Mosley (known as "Tom" to his friends) at one stage made a derogatory remark about the King, and Noel told me that he and his wife left the table immediately, and made for home. I mention this because there appears to be a "whitewash" of Mosley - he was from every point of view not a "normal" politician with a rebellious streak as an ex-Labour M.P. but a thoroughly nasty piece of work.

* * * * *

When a nephew married in Scotland, the reception was a sit-down breakfast and I found myself next to a young woman who was, plainly, a Scottish nationalist, although for her livelihood she worked during the week in London. This in itself struck me as a little incongruous, and during the interminably long pauses caused by the caterers she said, *apropos* of nothing, "Our money comes from slavery. I shall never see you again, so I can tell you this."

Some years before that, I had had luncheon with a barrister called Billy Strachan. He told me something of his early life: when in 1939 or 1940, without the knowledge or consent of his parents, and against their wishes, and with hardly a pound in his pocket, he had left Jamaica on a banana boat, bound for England. He was the son or grandson of a former Attorney-General in Jamaica, and he came to volunteer to fight for the UK; quite by chance (literally) and down to his last few pence he found himself outside the Air Ministry building in Kingsway, and thereafter his life really belongs to legend. He trained as a bomber pilot, went on 37 missions, and survived. (On his last mission he was severely wounded in the thigh or leg, but made it back to base with crew intact.) When on a bombing run and caught in searchlights, he would dive steeply, which was not too popular with his crew, as the contents of the latrine bucket would be spilled over - but he and they all survived.

He was descended from slaves - his great-grandmother, he told me, had been raped by the plantation owner, and in his immediate family, because he had the lightest colouring, the family money was invested in him so that he had the finest education and therefore the best opportunity to succeed.

At the end of the War, he had a wife (and I believe their first child) and no money. Therefore he went to the aircraft manufacturers whose planes during the War he had flown; where the manager he saw was someone he knew well and had flown with. They reminisced about the War, and then Billy said he had come for a job. The manager was very embarrassed, and said all he could offer Billy was a job sweeping the floors of the factory.

Billy came away deeply hurt; however, he read the appointments vacant column in the local paper and although he knew nothing about accountancy, he applied for a job as a book-keeper - he got it; it was a Thursday, and he had to start the following Monday. He went to W.H. Smith and bought two cheap books on book-keeping, and when he started work on the following Monday, he was able to get by. Ultimately, he went to the old London county council, and became a barrister and then a Magistrates' Clerk in a London court. He told me years later that I was the first "white" person to invite him to luncheon (naturally at Simpsons') - that would have been about 1960 - and over the years he wrote a number of articles and textbooks: once he told me that at one stage it had seemed as if he had been destined to be the first "ethnic minority" stipendiary magistrate but that it had not happened. He also told me (and I think this was on the very last occasion I met him) that he hoped to get to Scotland to visit his ancestral home. (Slaves of the estates in the West Indies took the name of their owner - in his case the Strachans who had given their name to the estate, and Strachans came from Scotland).

Well, I hope he got there, and I hope that he met the young lady who told me "We got our money from the slave trade." But real life isn't like that.

I read somewhere that a film was to be made of Billy's life - the only problem would have been that he was larger than life.

* * * * *

Billy Strachan's attitude on being offered the job of sweeping the floors is something completely understandable. However, I should mention another acquaintance of mine (this time, white not black) who by the end of the War had also attained the rank of squadron leader. His group captain was a man of some considerable private wealth (I suspect he had taken a short cut and married a rich wife), he was the chairman of a very old-established publishing company, and among other things was the owner of a farm. My friend approached him for a job and a cottage (for his house had been bombed in the War). "Yes," said his group-captain, "I'll let you have a cottage and give you a job, but on condition that you and your wife serve at table and help in my house at weekends." He accepted the terms (which I mention to show that colour at that time was not always a guide to a better job) and subsequently became managing director of the firm; he got involved in a whole raft of things outside publishing, and I recall he once offered me a 12-storey office block in Liverpool for £5.00. Yes, £5.00. This was when the "looney left" was in charge, and to have taken it over would have been made responsible for the rates on an empty and unlettable building, for who on earth would have wanted to invest in Liverpool at that time? Naturally, I did not take him up on his offer - an offer which was made in a jocular spirit (but I got the impression he would have gone through with it; understandably he was eager to be rid of the building).

* * * * *

I was having luncheon with Neville Cusworth, the then Chief Executive of Butterworths, in the Savoy Grill, who told me that that very morning he had had to order the destruction of all copies of Lord Denning's autobiography. What had happened, apparently, was that Denning (probably the greatest of the Common Law Judges of the 20th Century) had included two pages which discussed colour - anyone who knew Denning even remotely, would know that this delightful man had not a racist thought in his head, yet a barrister, Rudy Narayen, who was subsequently disbarred for unprofessional conduct not connected in any way with the Denning autobiography, accused him of racism. Because of course the copies were pulped, there is no means by which I could know what had been written, but I think it was a few sentences on juries which most people, in the climate of those days, would have regarded as harmless. But not Narayen - who used publicity as a very valuable tool in any set of circumstances. Anyway, as Neville said, any publisher in the land would have felt safe in publishing Denning. And Denning felt so shocked by it all that although being the last surviving Law Lord with no fixed retirement age, he deemed it appropriate to retire immediately.

* * * * *

Scene: The Imperial Hotel, Blackpool. Time: Friday evening. Occasion: The Annual Dinner of the then 150 (and plus) year-old Justices' Clerks' Society. I travelled to Blackpool for the annual meeting of the Society to which some years before I had been elected an honorary life member - an honour which I deeply valued and value still. I enjoy more than any other event of the legal year the Society's Council Dinner in London - generally held at the Law Society or in the halls of one or other of the Inns of Court - chosen on the current president's own professional background - where generally everyone who is anyone in the legal world from the Lord Chancellor or Lord Chief Justice down, is present. An unusual feature about the Dinner is the rule: no speeches.

The Annual Dinner of the Society, as distinct from that of its Council (in this particular year, at Blackpool) was also always a delightful occasion because it was held in various parts of the country for *all* members and their wives, and there were so many old friends present, but then, on this annual occasion, speeches are aplenty.

On this occasion after an excellent dinner, we settled down to the speeches. The Guest of Honour was Mr. Justice Caulfield - the chap who sprang into national prominence when Mr. Jeffrey Archer (as he then was and appears as if he will be again) sued a newspaper for what has subsequently become a celebrated libel case, and the learned Judge spoke of one of the witnesses - Mrs. Archer - as "fragrant". [As everyone now knows, Archer was subsequently found guilty of perjury at the trial, and sent down for four years in 2001.]

Caulfield began reasonably enough, by saying that when he had arrived he was mistaken initially by the hotel staff as a member of a jazz group they were expecting; that in his room, the bath had been left at shower, so that when he turned it on, while still clothed, in preparation for a bath, he was drenched by it. After a good dinner, it sounded better than it reads here - then he went on to say he had looked down the guest list to see who precisely he was thanking the hosts for in relation to the dinner; he had seen the name of the Mayor of Blackpool on the list - "the biggest crook I know". I do not know what everyone else thought, but I thought that they must be pretty good friends for him to make a remark of that kind at a public dinner with about 190 people present.

And then it came to my turn. Whereas the mayor had had to force a smile at a one liner, in my case it went on and on - on entry to the hotel, he said, there was a massive stand with books on Police Law, Magistrates' Law, Criminal Law, Local Government Law and every other kind of bloody law. (*This was at a period of my life when, having semi-relinquished editing the J.P. after 30 years, I did not have enough to do, so I began publishing books and organizing courses for lawyers and magistrates.*) He continued, now I've looked up Barry Rose in *Who's Who,* and he there says his recreation is entertaining people (not true -

entertaining and being entertained - a vastly different meaning) and you look him up when you're in Chichester, and ask him to entertain you. It's your money, and he went on in this vein for about four or five minutes. It was, for me, highly embarrassing - and I imagine it was equally so for the other 190 or so people present. By then, I had been in the political rough and tumble for many a long year, but I have never, ever, had to withstand such a concerted, personal and blistering attack: thank goodness, my memory has been good to me and I've forgotten most of the phraseology, but it really was nasty. That it was from someone whom I had never known before seemed to make it all the worse. He sat down, I imagine to the relief of most those there, and then the next speaker, Sir Desmond Heap, a former comptroller of the City of London and subsequently President of the Law Society, rose to speak and he went on for about four or five minutes *extolling* my virtues, and saying he and I had been friends for many years and it was completely wrong, etc., etc. From my point of view, it did much to neutralise what the learned Judge had said (Desmond told me afterwards that when he heard this attack being made on me, and he saw that I had no right of reply, it wasn't fair and had to be put right: his own prepared speech for the evening had to be thrown out of the window). What the guests thought I have no means of knowing - but I imagine that for virtually the whole of the speech slot to be taken up discussing someone most didn't know must have been disappointing.

Subsequently, we who were the special guests of the Society went into the hospitality suite, and there I saw the Judge. I went to him and said, "Sir, my name is Barry Rose. What you said was clearly actionable. Can I have the name of your solicitors who will accept service on your behalf." I must say that seemed to stop him in his tracks. He literally put his head between his hands, and again, quite literally, turned his face to the wall. He said, "Oh dear. The Lord Chancellor will hear of this."

I had a little knowledge of the likely cost of actions of this kind, and no way would I have commenced one - so in the end we had a drink together. I think what had caused the outburst was that (as a member of the Society told me who knew him from the days when he had been on the Northern Circuit) he had received a few weeks earlier an invitation from me to the dinner to mark the 150th Anniversary of the *Justice of the Peace Reports* - I had invited those members of the Judiciary of those Divisions of the High Court involved in the subject matter of those *Reports*. It was to be a white tie affair at Stationers' Hall, and as it happened, so many Judges accepted the invitation (a much higher percentage than I had anticipated) that some especial friends could not be accommodated (I think the seating capacity was 56 or something like that). The type of printing I used was the old-fashioned but very expensive die-stamped kind, and each invitation was personally inscribed in an elegant "olde-type" of hand-writing. Although he had not come, he seemed particularly impressed by this, and obviously thought I must be mega-rich to spend so much money on invitation cards and a dinner of this kind.

A person who had known Caulfield and who was at the Dinner, told me his father had been a docker, and he had come up really the hard way: he thought that there was a teeny-weeny chip on his shoulder; he also told me that the day he had been appointed a Judge, his wife walked out on him. So one way or another, he was a colourful figure in Liverpool; my informant told me that I must always remember that Liverpool was not English; I suppose rather like Dublin not being Irish.

It was years before I plucked up courage to attend a further Annual Dinner of the Society.

Gavin Thurston (*q.v.*) was Coroner for Westminster; he wrote prodigiously on medico-legal matters for me for many years, and at that time, books for others. He also wanted me to be a member of the Authors' Club, of which he was chairman. The club's premises in Whitehall Court were small, but really had everything that anyone could desire of his club - cuisine linked to that of Whitehall Court as was accommodation - there was a marvellous view across the Thames, and the most delightful membership - small in numbers, which had the advantage that everyone knew everyone and all sharing a common interest in the written word. Gavin had a book, *Coronership*, which he offered me in terms rather like these: "You won't make any money out of it; Butterworths have turned it down - but you should sell 230 copies or so. I don't want you to lose money, so please turn it down if you're not happy about its prospects." Well, I printed 600-odd copies, and it sold out, and I think it would be true to say it stimulated a greater interest in Coroners' Law which at that particular time had not perhaps been receiving the attention it deserved.

Although by the time I knew him, he was Coroner for Westminster, he started life as a humble general practitioner in Essex (and one of the partners in the practice was, coincidentally, Ernest Anthony (*q.v.*)). Gavin told me that he had sent out a questionnaire to the practice's patients on their sex lives, "And do you know, Barry, only 84 per cent ever had sex. Just think of it: 16 out of every hundred just not interested in it." This was much less complicated than the *Kinsey Report* published about 20 or 30 years later, but Gavin really could have claimed to have been the originator of such surveys (although naturally, on a very limited basis).

Alas, the lease of the Authors' expired, and the club as a temporary expedient was forced to move a few yards down the road as 'guests' of the National Liberal Club. It certainly was not

136

the same, and as I could not countenance the politics of the National Liberal Club, or eating and drinking under the busts of various past Liberal politicians I resigned, which was when I became a member of the Oxford and Cambridge University Club - then rather an intimate club until its merger with the United University, which brought with it a dowry enabling its previous air of genteel shabbiness to be replaced by luscious new furnishings and decorations. But it ceased to be the same club; that, however, is another story. The Authors' has long since moved in with the Arts Club in Dover Street, but other than as a guest, I have never gone back.

Some years later, Gavin Thurston was having dinner with me at the Garrick and told me of treatment he was having for a particular condition and the curious effect it was having upon him - for example, he had no interest in sex, and remarked philosophically that he reckoned he had eight years left. He left the table for the usual reason; whilst he was away, a man opposite me said he was a surgeon and knew my guest - he had overheard the conversation, but sadly, he said, my guest did not have eight years, but six months at the most. Alas, he was right. Gavin was greatly interested in all matters relating to people - he told me once (this at a time when Coroners had to view bodies prior to the inquest) that the smell of death he found not unpleasing; his observations on the suicide of Sir Bernard Spilsbury, said to be the greatest pathologist of his time, that "conscience" had been the cause - he had, as an "Expert Witness", sent so many innocent people to the gallows.

* * * * *

Ernest Anthony was a doctor in general practice, and a magistrate. He wrote a handbook (in conjunction with a learned Clerk, C.J. Berryman) on the law affecting, and duties of, magistrates, which

Butterworths published on an annual basis and which I believe still do. He expressed a desire to meet me as editor of the *J.P.*

I signed him up to write a "From Court 4 ..." column. He loved controversy, and practically each week would come out with some outspoken views on the law and those administering it.

I think it would be fair to say that in some respects he was regarded by some as a sort of Alf Garnet of the magistrates' courts - but controversy is the lifeblood of a journal, and people would read his column just to say how awful it was (or how he had put his finger on a particular matter). He had his supporters and he had his detractors. And of course, there were plenty of other contributors and correspondents prepared to cross swords with him so if anyone believed in a free press such a column should occasion no problem. As he was a magistrate and a doctor, this seemed to be the combination that the national press liked, and almost every week, his comments were picked up and broadcast to a wider public. For a specialised journal, such publicity never helped in the slightest respect in terms of circulation, etc., but I think it gave other contributors a feeling of pleasure that the journal they were writing for was attracting notice in the wider world outside.

Anthony was an extraordinary chap; his family immigrated at the end of the first World War from (I believe) Lithuania, and his energy was prodigious. He succeeded Dr. Charles Hill as "The Radio Doctor" a doctor who spoke on medical problems for 15 minutes on the radio each morning. (Although not germane to the story, Hill subsequently went into politics, and "his friendly reassuring voice" was credited with having won - as a result of a single Conservative Political Broadcast - the General Election of the time, when he was used to counter "the friendly reassuring voice" of J.B. Priestley of a previous broadcast, in a piece called "Chuck it Priestley" generally credited by many political journalists as the reason why Labour lost that particular General Election.) Anthony did the B.B.C. stint for six-and-a-half years and wrote a number of medical books for lay people as well as contributing to the writing of law books; he ran a column of advice for the readers of a 'teen' magazine. "You know, Barry, those letters are not made up ... they're real" and as a hobby, he made jewellery and tablecloths. Therefore, a considerable man - and he told me how, during the War, he had been attached to Tangmere, the fighter station of the R.A.F. close to Chichester, and as he was a medical officer (not on "ops") his wife was able to come down and spend some weekends at the *Ship Hotel*. He was having luncheon one Sunday with her, and noticed that nearby a man was reading a Sunday newspaper upside down. He went to a telephone; the man was taken away for questioning, and Ernest subsequently heard he had been shot as a spy.

His career with me ended on a low note. I received an invitation from someone in the Lord Chancellor's Department for luncheon in the House of Lords; I went, but another person in the Department ambushed me first and said the writings of Dr. Anthony were causing some anxiety: what if his expressed views were taken to appeal on an unrelated case on which he had adjudicated? It would be very embarrassing if he had to be dropped from the Commission of the Peace and that would be the position if the articles continued. I had previously decided to retire from editing the *J.P.* (moving myself up to editor-in-chief, a move which becomes quite meaningless when the ownership of the journal had become the same) after 30 years - that 30 years would be up at the end of December, but I wanted there to be a neat and tidy termination of my stint. My deputy, John Edye, was to take over; he was no admirer of Ernest Anthony, and week after week would fulminate to me against him; he would come into my office, brandish that week's offending piece, and then, in simulated rage, put it on the floor and jump on it to indicate his great displeasure. Dear John. And when he became editor, he declared, he would get rid of Anthony; naturally, however, when he heard the report of my "chance" meeting in the Department - Anthony must stay, at least for a decent period - which he did, for about another three or four months. Even John, with his dislike of Ernest Anthony's opinions as expressed in his articles, must never be thought for a moment to lose his independence of action at the behest of the Lord Chancellor's Office.

* * * * *

El Vino's in Fleet Street was an establishment much used by me in my salad days. It was presided over by Norman Bower, who dressed in a morning coat and invariably had a rose in his buttonhole. He ran a tight ship; the story was told of him that someone had gone into his bar looking very fragile, and had asked for a Firna Branca - "Don't stock that foreign muck in here; you'll have a brandy and soda like the rest of us." But it was (as it still is) a lovely bar and although it keeps the Bar there, it certainly misses the journalists who also used it in strength when Fleet Street was truly the Street of Adventure and not, as it chooses to do now, call itself the Street of Shame.

It had the tradition that no lady was allowed to stand at the bar but had to sit at one of the side tables. On literally dozens of occasions, I would enter with a woman when I had a London office, and if there was no free chair, immediately a man would give up a table so that she could sit. I think we all know how embarrassing and worse it can be when women are jostled when in close proximity to men, especially in bars, and the Management insisted upon the rule. The sex equality brigade took them to court; I was told it cost *El Vino's* £24,000 (and this was many years ago) to fight the case on the principle of the thing. It lost. Now it has a strict dress code, and the sex "equality" people are seen there no more.

Sir David Mitchell, M.P., a former Minister of State for Transport, was a member of the family owning *El Vino's*, and we were invited to the wedding reception of his daughter to the son of one of Jean's friends. Fellow guests included Enoch Powell and his wife: it was shortly after the Falklands' conflict, and the description he gave of Margaret Thatcher in the House of not being the Iron Lady but of truly forged steel was happily phrased. He expressed pleasure when I complimented him upon his choice of words.[1]

We then talked about his Rivers of Blood speech, which had resulted in his dismissal by Edward Heath from the Opposition Front Bench and, ultimately, his resignation from the Conservative Party to spend the rest of his life in the political wilderness (although he represented an Ulster constituency for a number of years as a Unionist). He told me he was surprised by the furore his speech had caused: he was accused of having made it without consulting anyone in the Party, but he told me he had sent it in the usual form to the Midlands Central Office Chief Agent before delivery, who sent it back approved, with the words "Needs to be said" or something like that. Students of political history should

---

1. The exact phraseology as recorded in *Hansard*, is as follows: "Is the Rt. Hon. Lady aware that the report on June 17, two days after the victory, has now been received from the public analyst on a certain substance recently subject to analysis and that I have received a copy of the report? It shows that the substance in the test consisted of ferrous matter of the highest quality, that is of exceptional tensile strength, and is highly resistant to wear and tear and to stress, and may be used with advantage for all national purposes?"

note this - since Edward Heath had wrongly said it had been delivered without warning (although I am not suggesting this was said deliberately to mislead).

Bearing in mind the intellectual quality of Powell, where he outshone Heath at every turn - I have always suspected that the opportunity was seized upon to get rid of him as a possible contender for the leadership, although it must be said that in the earlier election of leader, Powell did not do well in the number of votes cast for him. Powell said to me, with malicious pleasure, that at any rate he had cost Heath the Midlands vote. But then, Powell was much too "big" to be malicious about anything or anybody - so I withdraw that word.

I had first met him at the Conservative College of the North before the 1950 general election - where I was able to correct him on some minor point - the nature of the man was that he accepted the correction immediately; years later I was having luncheon at the members' table of the Athenaeum: I reminded him that the last time we had met had been on the platform of the Rex Ballroom at Bognor, when he had spoken to the largest political meeting ever to be held in that town - over 830 people. "Ah," he said sadly, "I couldn't pull them in like that today." I am still rather proud at having presided over that meeting: it made the lead story in the *Daily Telegraph* the following morning.

* * * * *

As a generalisation, it sometimes seems to me that many women enjoy playing with fire. I recall travelling to London by chance in the company of the vice-chairman (women) of the Chichester Divisional Conservative Association; as we neared London, she said I was going to be surprised by the person who would be waiting for her at the barrier. I guessed it would be a boyfriend, and frankly, I did not want to know - so I made my apologies for dashing away and, without looking left or right, scurried for a taxi. I was thus never to see who it was she was meeting.

She was a lovely person, wholly undeserving of what was to happen to her. Her husband was a member of the Chichester City Council (in those days prior to the 1972 reorganisation, before its diminution to its present parish council status following a yet further reorganisation) and was chairman of its housing committee. She herself had a business disaster which I imagine was the principal reason why she and her husband needed, in the first place, to apply for a joint mortgage to the local authority on the house they lived in. In accordance with standard procedure, the house would have been valued by the city surveyor, and the grant of the mortgage would be against the value of the house. The city council would have loaned the money, and borrowed from the Public Works Loans Board at a fractionally lower rate of interest - so that the worthy burgesses of the City of Chichester would not have been out of pocket and the only losers would have been the building societies in not getting the business. (The Act under which it was done was post 1914-1918 War, to assist in the better housing of the country. As an Act of Parliament, it suffered from the defect that it was never - or very rarely - advertised, whereas the building societies not only advertised continuously, but had high street shops etc. specialising in just this one thing.) When the item came before the committee, the chairman vacated the chair lest it might have been argued that the rubber-stamping of the application - for that is what it amounted to - gave him an unfair pecuniary advantage contrary to section 72 of the Local Government Act 1933, and would have left the room for the item to be discussed in his absence, as was customary. Everything honourable and above board.

However, also on the Committee was to be found the person (whom I suspect was he who would have been waiting at the barrier at Victoria Station some time before - anyway, by this time, it was fairly common knowledge that my vice-chairman had a lover). He did not withdraw; indeed, why should he? He had no pecuniary interest in the property at all. But this chap was not only a member of the city council but also a considerable force in local politics - he was, in my opinion, a particularly valuable and fearless member of the county council - fearless in the sense that he was not frightened to say unpopular things, and also had the time to research matters about which he intended to speak.

In the result all three were arrested; my vice chairman resigned immediately so that her continued presence in the list of officers should not embarrass the Party. When the case came before the Chichester Magistrates' Court, the "boyfriend" had the case thrown out. (He had come to me for my opinion, and I gave it - I was so astonished to hear his story that I thought he could not be telling me the truth, but on the basis he was, there was simply no case. Prosecuted? It didn't make sense.) At the magistrates' court hearing he was represented by a silk - the court instantly dismissed the charges; the other defendants had legal aid and were committed to Lewes Assizes, when the Judge somewhat irritably dismissed the charges, wondering why they had been brought. It was an absolute disgrace that the lives of these people, who had done much honourable work in the public service, should have their lives so wantonly wrecked in this manner, because inevitably all became unelectable - on the public perception that there can be no smoke without fire.

* * * * *

As for me, some time later I wanted a telephone link between two offices on opposite sides of the same road: British Telecom quoted a huge figure which no doubt for technical reasons was perfectly correct - so we went to the private sector to see what they could offer. I was in London, and a colleague phoned me to say that rather than digging up the surface of the road to put the link in this way - why not go overhead? Warning bells jingled in my head - "Be sure to get the consent of the council before they start work on this," I said. My mistake was that I had not specified *which* council. My colleague reported that the *county* council said there was no problem; we would have to pay a wayleave of £20 per annum. So on that basis we went ahead - whereupon the Chichester *City* Council said my company was in breach of lack of planning consent and must remove it immediately. I argued that it was *de minimus*, the council said it was not, and insisted upon its removal. In the end the local radio interviewed me, an interview which was heard by our friend who had found himself prosecuted basically, as seemed to me, for being the lover of the wife of the chairman of the housing committee (see previous page). In one afternoon, he found 13 or 14 city council premises where there were overhead telephone lines between offices. Truly, there is one law for us, and one law for "them at the council". I suspect he thought he was repaying me for my stalwart support of him earlier - but it was good of him in any event. And the council's overhead lines vanished as if by magic; even although no longer on the city council, one imagines he still wielded considerable clout.

* * * * *

In the meantime, in place of my lady vice-chairman who had so honourably stood down, Mrs. "Cindy" Andrew Montague-

Douglas-Scott was elected. She too, was a lovely person. Possibly as a result of her and her husband's social and family connections, Sir Alec Douglas-Home came to speak to us at a dinner at Bognor. My memory tells me that over 200 came to this - the most expensive (and most successful) fund-raising dinner in the constituency's history, and was held at the Rex Ballroom - in my time a venue also used for Enoch Powell. (The Rex Ballroom was demolished as a result of comprehensive redevelopment, *q.v.*).

Sir Alec, in explaining to me the poor representation of the Conservative Party in Scotland, said that their principal difficulty was in getting people to accept constituency office, in other words, to be party activists.

Having held party office as an 'activist' during the time of Churchill, Eden, MacMillan, Heath and Thatcher, I must say Alec Douglas-Home made a refreshing change and came pretty well near the top, of course excluding Churchill. To be next to someone for about two or three hours, who actually had met Hitler, meant I should have been bursting with questions - but as it was, I completely forgot as I listened whilst he spoke on various aspects of country pursuits and of his constituency and the Border Country before he began his speech. A wholly delightful person.

* * * * *

There is, or should be, complete confidentiality between patient and doctor. Bill Loveys was not only my friend, but also Member of Parliament for Chichester. As everyone knows, fighting an election is an expensive business, and when I became chairman, I said to John Pitt, the Agent (never suspecting for a moment that healthwise anything was the matter with Loveys) that it would be prudent to insure against the necessity of a by-election during the term of the Parliament. I was thinking particularly of death or incapacity caused by accident - car, air, train - that sort of thing; his health never troubled me in the slightest (I knew Loveys's father and had I thought of Bill's health in general terms, I would have said - bearing in mind his farming background that he came of good country stock). But then, in terms of strictest secrecy - when we were off to lunch to a pub in Singleton - he revealed to me that he could have a heart attack at any moment. I must say I felt a degree of apprehension, seated as I was in his powerful Jag - but when we sat down to luncheon, he told me his mother had collapsed and died suddenly in the kitchen, and that although if he lived another 10 years, treatment of his particular condition would have advanced and the medics had told him they would be able to do something about it - but in the meantime nothing could be done; if I agreed, he would like to continue sitting as an M.P. until the next General Election. Of course I agreed (and he said, coincidentally, that he wished me to succeed him - you and I, Barry, are the only people I know who can speak to dukes and dustmen on equal terms). But what he had revealed to me was absolutely top secret; no one was to know.

Then, Patrick Doherty (the relatively newly appointed constituency agent) about a week or fortnight later said he had heard rumours concerning Bill's health, had I heard anything? Naturally, I could say nothing. Then the Treasurer, Air Vice Marshall Langford-Sainsbury, told me he had been speaking to a local heart specialist, who had told him that he (the specialist) had attended a seminar in London the previous week, and there one of the speakers had spoken of "an interesting congenital heart condition - it belonged to the Member of Parliament for Chichester". Naturally, I could still say nothing, and whether Bill ever found out about this appalling breach of professional etiquette, I was never to know. He was due to have luncheon with me the very day he died - when, according to his own prediction, he collapsed without warning - and when I probably would have told him.

* * * * *

I was at Scarborough for yet another Conservative Annual Conference. I had not known whether I could get away for part of that week, and thus had made no advance arrangements; when I discovered I could, I merely suggested to my then secretary that she phoned the hotels in alphabetical order, to find one with a free room - for the whole of Scarborough was filled by the Conference delegates. As a result, on arrival and inquiring for the situation of the bar, I was told, "The bar, Sir? This is a temperance hotel." So I smartly gravitated to the Grand Hotel - which at that time was said to have the longest bar in Europe; with the Conservatives in Scarborough, it was needed to have. I found our Parliamentary Correspondent, Jim Murray, and we were having a quiet drink when the door opened. Suddenly, almost magically, the whole room - there must have been over 200 present - fell silent. Randolph Churchill came in. With the room still silent, he went to Selwyn Lloyd (with Eden, one of the people involved in the Suez adventure) who was later to become Speaker of the House of Commons and said with the clarity that all of us heard in the bar. "Selwyn - the worst foreign secretary we've had since Castlereigh."[1] And Selwyn Lloyd replied, "I am obliged to you for your opinion, Randolph." And that was all - the noise of the bar resumed as if nothing had been said.

---

1. When Randolph Churchill was admitted into hospital for a check-up, the hospital issued a statement saying that the examination had found nothing 'malignant' in his condition. Evelyn Waugh said, "How clever of them to find the only part of Randolph that is not malignant." It seemed an appropriate comment.

Charles Arnold-Baker is a chap with a fascinating history, whom I got to know shortly after the end of the war, and with whom (at one stage) I was going into partnership in a publishing enterprise. (We both thought that it was essential that the chemistry should also be right between our two families - and they were to come down to Bognor one Sunday for luncheon. On that very morning, however, Charles was rushed into hospital dangerously ill with meningitis from which he took six months or so to recover - thus, our joint adventure never proceeded.) However, I should take matters in proper sequence. Although he does not use the title, he is the son of a German baron of ancient lineage (the title dates from 1140, the oldest surviving nobleman's family from Prussia, and for good measure, he is a descendant of Charlemagne); his parents were divorced and his family moved to England. It is almost impossible to visualise a more English background: Winchester and Magdalen College, Oxford, followed by the Admiralty Bar. But he had been born in Germany, which would have been the important thing in the event of capture, and I suppose he could have been executed as a traitor in fighting for Britain. One of his war-time tasks was to head a small body of men who guarded Winston Churchill at Chartwell against a possible "snatch" group from the air; he told me that he would be invited to dinner - but there would rarely be much conversation as the Great Man would be reading, generally a book on military history or "The Dynasts".

As for his period at the Bar I suspect there was not too much work about at that time, and he entered local government at a national level. For the infamous 1972 Local Government Act, he was responsible for the only part of local government to be salvaged intact from the wreckage. It was in the context of the National Association of Parish Councils (later to be the Association of Local Councils) that I first met him, then later when he became a member of the court of management of the Association of Councillors. Local Government Law is, I suppose, his main speciality - but he ranges over such a wide field it could be anything: he is a true polymath. One Sunday afternoon, for example, by chance I heard him on Radio Four reading his autobiography which seemed to cover an astonishingly wide range of activity, including the editorship of one of my journals and the job of a Road Transport Commissioner, and a professor of law at the City of London University. Probably many of those who read this book are acquainted with Dr. Brewer's *Dictionary of Phrase and Fable*. *Brewer* is now Big Business and in its umpteenth edition, Arnold Baker's *Companion to British History* is in my opinion an infinitely superior work - it took him some 30-odd years to write. Somehow, it has never caught on - I hope someone, somewhere, takes it on board. It is truly a remarkable book: part dictionary; part encyclopaedia; part picker-up of unconsidered trifles - but wholly delightful as a work of reference.

One evening in late November or early December it was snowing and I found myself in Fleet Street. I saw Charles coming out of El Vino's (he lives in The Temple, bordering Fleet Street). His wife was away from home, concluding I gathered, the purchase of some property in Italy. He had been in the off-licence section of El Vino's; naturally, I suggested we both went into the bar. Although he protested that he had no tie on, he was muffled against the cold and it was not noticeable to the naked eye that he was - according to the tenets of the place - improperly dressed. So, against his better judgement, I marched him back into the place, but the bar functionary refused to serve us on the grounds that he lacked a tie. Of course, she was absolutely right in applying the rules, although how she managed to detect that he was not wearing one, was a wonder to me - so we had to march out again, to the

"Cock" along the road. So there we have it: an Officer of the Order of the British Empire; a member of the Bar; a Brain of Britain (so it was whispered - but never by himself), a Professor of Law at the City of London University; the author of numerous books on law and society, and the author of a remarkable reference book which will be remembered and used for a very long time by those fortunate enough to possess a copy - turned away because he was not wearing a tie.

* * * * *

Joe Yahuda was one of the diminishing band of barristers who operated on the cab rank principle at the Old Bailey, where barristers were available to help indigent defendants who, otherwise, had no 'brief' to defend them. Those awaiting trial would point to the one they fancied, and thereafter the barrister was to give of his best for the sake of the impecunious client, and to be paid an insignificant sum for his trouble. The experience gained, however, was valuable to the newly called barrister. (This was in the time of Poor Prisoners' Defence, and Legal Aid had not then emerged upon the scene). Joe was a small man in stature, but he had a big heart; he was to tell me many things about the Jewish faith - such as one gained brownie points if, on Holy Days, you *walked* to the synagogue - thus, the Great Eastern Hotel (opposite Liverpool Street Station) was always full on the eve of Holy Days as the walk to the synagogue in the City of London was a comparatively short one for those who were elderly and who otherwise on any other day would have summoned their chauffeur-driven second Roller. Joe was a delightful man, but he had a flaw - he was teetotal. He told me early on in our friendship that he had this unfortunate perversion, but that his wife had insisted on keeping wines and spirits to enable them to show hospitality to callers. He told me that the day he returned from her funeral, he poured the contents of all the bottles down the sink, such was his hatred of alcohol. Well.

Despite such an admission, I remained on friendly terms, so much so that when he celebrated something of some significance the Inn of which he was a member, broke the flag over it in his honour, and he invited me to Sunday luncheon at the Inn as his guest where he had been asked to preside; alas, an invitation I had to decline - presumably the honour accorded to him was either on account of his age, or the anniversary of date of his call. He told me his father was a bookseller in Cairo (the New Testament kept in a locked cupboard, to which he was forbidden access) and he had come to England in the early 1920s being called to the Bar in 1932 or thereabouts.

He took a great liking to my then secretary - a comely young lady of some 21 or 22 summers, who asked me to act as her chaperone - rather wisely, as I perceived from his behaviour towards her even in my presence. Ultimately, she was to write to him to say she could no longer see him, as she was engaged to someone else. Whether this was responsible for what then happened or not, I do not know - but I do know that he seemed to take a liking for alcohol at that time; whether or not he regretted pouring down the drain his previous stock, I never knew.

Looking back upon this somewhat bizarre period of my life, when I used to take them to my haunts such as Simpsons and one of my clubs, and he responded by inviting her (with me tagging along) to the Authors' - incorporated in the Arts - I reflect upon how lonely a man can become, and wonder if someone will ever find it necessary to be chaperoned because of me!

Diana (my daughter) is now a member of the Reform (the Reform being one of the first "gentlemen's clubs" to have admitted women). Charles Scholefield, a former solicitor who switched to become a barrister (he later became a silk) had been chairman of the Club committee for deciding such things, and gave his opinion that the rules required no alteration to permit it to admit women, as when it was founded there had been no mention of gender at all, so that both sexes were equally able to join.

Charles spent most of his professional life on Private Street Works cases which may seem odd, but he explained to me that there was quite a lot of money in it, which when you considered the cost of an average road improvement scheme, was obvious. I suppose Planning Law has all but eliminated the need for such cases today, where the planning consent for a new estate would include the provision of a built-up road, in most cases. Charles became the legal editor of *Local Government Review*; he and four others with myself formed the editorial board of the *Review* and we would meet monthly in J.P.L. Griffiths' room at the London School of Economics, where we had some wine, before going on to dine at Simpsons' just across the way. One evening, having finished dinner, Charles asked if he could share my cab to Victoria - he had to travel to Brighton whilst I would be going to Bognor. Victoria Station was a shambles; it was being rebuilt, and there were unlit parts of the platform which was in the process of being resurfaced. We parted; I to go to Platform 13, he to Platform 17. He tripped and fell. He was over 80 at this time, and in falling broke his thigh in three separate places. He wore a Homburg hat; he was about 6'3" tall, and looked every inch the eminent (if elderly) silk that he was. Because he suffered from a hiatus hernia, alone of all of us, he had had nothing to drink except water - yet the Railway Police coming across this elderly gentleman writhing in pain on the concourse, accused him of being drunk and disorderly. The Police. Ah, yes, the Police.

It was in the era of punks/rockers/teddy boys - I was never quite sure which was which, and four of these young men deliberately lost their (same) Brighton train to look after him until help arrived in the shape of an ambulance which took him to Westminster hospital. When I heard about the accident, I was very distressed because he had only come up from Brighton for the meeting, and it seemed all my fault. However, he recovered in due course, although in the process, his wife left him. His uncle, Sir Joshua Scholefield, had been one of my predecessors, as editor of the *J.P.* in the 1920s, and he, Charles, was responsible for the most remarkable legal work (apart from *Halsbury*) that I have known: Lumley's *Public Health Acts* - a truly tremendous work of eight volumes, and each containing an astonishing wealth of material.

He did so much work for various Bar sub-committees such as training and ethics; he did so much work for Butterworths; he did so much work for the Masonic Movement (he was also a leading light in the Sherlock Holmes Society), and all in all was a delightful man. When he died, I appeared to be the only non-family present at the funeral; frankly, I thought it was rather a poor show - but, of course, there may have been a memorial service and I might have missed it in the "announcements" columns.

I remember a luncheon party at his house on the outskirts of Brighton - apart from myself, a rather distinguished gathering, and it emerged that without exception all the men present did not drive and left this activity to their wives.

* * * * *

I have mentioned the Reform Club on more than one occasion. I had to go to London to meet Mr. John Moss, C.B.E., a barrister who was former Public Assistance Officer for Kent. Kent was always an extraordinary county - the Clerk in my younger days was W.L. Platts, who was so dominant and autocratic that he held some Kent county council committee meetings at the Athenaeum. John Moss may well have been minded to have done the same at the Reform (almost next door) - certainly, with the ending of the Poor Law, people like him were exceedingly valuable in the hand-over from local to national government. The day for my luncheon with him dawned fine, and my train was due to get in to Victoria Station at 12.45. It did, too, but what I had not calculated was that on that day, the King and Queen of Siam (Thailand) were to begin a State visit to this country - as a result, the Mall was closed to vehicular traffic, as were certain other roads as well - including the entry and exit areas of the Station itself. This had the effect of making all taxis unavailable. Still, it was a beautiful day, and what was wrong with a stiff walk down Buckingham Palace Road, turn left, and then right at St James's Palace, entry into Pall Mall and so to the Reform? Also, to be blessed as I walked, by martial music as the Royal Carriages followed, although catching up with me fast. The King of Thailand had (and presumably still has) a number of different titles including that of Emperor of the Golden Umbrella, and it must have seemed appropriate to him that as he reached Buckingham Palace with the Queen, an almost tropical downfall of rain should occur. Even to this day, I cannot remember where I sheltered - but partially shelter I did, sharing a shop blind in Pall Mall opposite St James's Palace, with dozens of others; however, not before I was thoroughly wet, like a half drowning animal, with my suit flapping around me - but look yonder, there was a taxi. I got it, and sank back with a squelch. "Reform Club," I said. "That's going to be difficult," he said, "all the roads are out of action at the moment, but I'll get you there."

About 10 minutes later, the cabbie pulled up and opened the door to the tropical storm still in full blast outside the cab. "Reform Club," he said. I paid him off, and drawing my jacket over my head and shoulders in the hope of warding off some of the rain, dashed up the steps. The hall porter looked disdainfully at this wet and dripping object in front of him, and inquired, civilly enough, the nature of my business. "Mr. John Moss," I gasped. His brow lightened. "Ah, yes, Sir," he said, "Mr. Moss has just gone into the Coffee Room. You know the way, of course." I nodded, and set off. I glanced round the room; it seemed vaguely different from the last time I was in the Reform; doubtless a few members relinquished their interest in what they were eating or drinking or saying, to glance at the apparition presented by my appearance, but of Mr. John Moss there was no sign. I returned to the porter. "Ah," he said, "was I mistaken, Sir?" and he forthwith ordered various minions to seek out Mr. John Moss in the Library, and in various other sanctuaries normally not known to non-members, but they all came back empty handed. There was no Mr. John Moss. "I was sure I saw him going into the Coffee Room, Sir. I'll see if I can find him."

A few minutes later, he came back with a puzzled looking gentleman in tow, and said, "Here you are, Sir." I declaimed, "That's not Mr. John Moss." "Which Club do you think you're in, Sir?" said the Porter. "The Reform." "No, Sir," he said silkily, "You're in the Travellers, next door." Ah, well. (My error was occasioned by the Club having - and still had, the last time I was in it - a poster as decoration declaiming REFORM - a strange poster if I may say so, to have in the Travellers' Club with the Reform Club next door - which I suppose disoriented me.)

On another occasion, I came out from luncheon at the

Travellers, and I perceived Sir Anthony Blunt, Sometime Keeper of the Queen's Pictures, unfrocked some weeks earlier as being involved in spying for the USSR. I was puzzled at seeing him there: I would have thought the Travellers would have expelled him from membership instantaneously; as it was, he got a cab before I did. Ah well, again.

* * * * *

In 1985 I received an invitation to become an honorary Life Fellow of the American Association of Criminology. Having ascertained that this surprising honour was merely an effort on their part to honour me and that they wanted no money for the privilege, I accepted. I accepted from my then personal address of "5 Wychwood Close, Craigwell-on-Sea." In due course I received the certificate. It was made out to S. Wychwood Close Esq. I still have it, and still think it brilliant on the part of the Post Office to have found me.

* * * * *

Herbert Brabin (Local Government Officer for the Conservative Party) told me once he had been head-hunted by Lord Woolton from the North West. He told me of the occasion (I think he said 1947, but it may have been a year or so later) when the Local Government Section of the Conservative Party was to be addressed by Winston Churchill - no less. I believe the venue was Earls Court. He (Brabin) and Woolton (chairman of the Party) stood outside, waiting for the great man to arrive - apparently, local government was then the (as some of us would say it is today!) Cinderella of the Conservative Party, consisting at Central Office of just Herbert and probably a shared secretary (perhaps an exaggeration, but not by much), so it was an extra special treat to have Winston address them. Herbert told me that Winston had said that he knew nothing about local government, and would he (Herbert) prepare something for him to say. You can imagine how Herbert toiled over that speech - and then as the Great Man stepped out of his car, he said to Woolton (with Brabin at this side), "we're not going to let the Beaver (pet name for Beaverbrook) get away with this." ('This' being some outlandish campaign launched by the *Daily Express* that very morning) and the speech so carefully prepared by Herbert was never, or at any rate, only partially, used - instead, Winston replied to Beaverbrook's latest broadside on the Empire or whatever it was.

* * * * *

It must not be thought that Winston was the only one to regard Local Government as beyond his own understanding - I was once chairman for Harold Wilson giving the G.W. Reynolds Memorial Lecture - a speech he had to read with such care which convinced me it was not his own speech at all but one that Joe Haines, his assiduous Press Secretary, had written.

It was, by the way, given at the former County Hall, when it was the home of the G.L.C. After the address, we had the better part of an hour's chat, as we were left alone by everyone else. A waiter with a tray and a bottle of Scotch stood by us, and by the time he (Harold Wilson) departed, it (the Scotch) was sadly depleted. It was only 12.45 (Scotch is not my drink, and I hadn't touched a drop). It was not only his memory which was extraordinary; his head was, too! He was indeed, a very engaging personality. His off-the-cuff remarks about various M.P.s of both parties (never malicious) showed an immense knowledge.

I remember with great affection Louis Heren; he was deputy editor of *The Times* when it was owned by Lord Thompson. He had a liking for Bloody Mary's - and he told me how he had acquired it. Lord Astor, who, after losing an estimated £54 million on this title, decided to sell it on and the Canadian multi-millionaire Lord Thompson bought it. Now Thompson was one of those who had pulled himself up by his own bootstraps, and owned a vast chain of newspapers and radio stations - he was very successful but of course eschewed the demon drink. Thus, when it was in his mind to extend his empire into China, he took Louis with him; he would meet the Chinese Prime Minister, for example, talk business for say 30 minutes, and then hand over to Louis for a newspaper interview. China is such a vast country, and Thompson was so thorough, that they found themselves flying over that country seemingly for days on end. Thompson being teetotal presented difficulties for Louis - thus, the deception of Bloody Mary's which *looked* harmless and had no smell of alcohol. Louis told me that at one stage, Thompson said, "Don't suppose you have ever seen a cheque for 50 million?" Louis agreed it would be a new experience - whereupon Thompson opened his wallet and produced a reproduction of a cheque for £50,000,000 [or it might have been dollars; I cannot remember] made out to his son. "Thought it about time the boy had a little money of his own."

I met Louis Heren shortly after a news item appeared - it related to the release of hitherto confidential memoranda under the '30 year rule'. It concerned Louis in this way: it had obviously been prepared by the 'spooks' of the Foreign Office, and cast doubt upon his motives in having written some stories concerning the East some 30 years before.

Well, you can libel someone who is dead to your heart's content - there is no remedy. But of course, Louis was still then very much alive, and his journalistic integrity was intact. I never saw him again, and never knew whether he sought his remedy - certainly, he should have done.

* * * * *

I went to London two or three times a week but almost invariably from Chichester at "gentlemen's hours". However, whenever I went by a "workers' train" - i.e., arriving Victoria 9-ish, I would invariably leave Bognor - where I lived - and hear people on adjoining seats gossiping about the members of the (then) Bognor Regis U.D.C. This gossip was quite outrageous - "I see Councillor X has bought himself a new car at our expense", or "Councillor Y is going up in the world - did you see where he is moving to?" etc. Very unpleasant. (Although out of sequence, I well remember my time on the Bognor Regis U.D.C. - apart from a free seat to the opening night of the Council's "Dazzle" concert party, we each paid 4d. (old money) for a cup of tea and a biscuit during committee meetings.)

At that time I was chairman of the Divisional Conservative Association for Chichester - Bognor was its largest constituent part. And of course, it was my duty as I conceived it to be, to keep the constituency Conservative. Thus it was I spoke to the Agent - my dear friend John Pitt, and said that it seemed to me I should see what things were really like on the Council - were they as bad as the gossipers on the train (and elsewhere) made out? John thought I was mad even to contemplate such a task (I was pretty fully engaged on the West Sussex County Council and in other directions), but being obstinate by nature when a by-election came up, I won the nomination and later, the seat. The council was "Independent" - which was all right so long as it was well run - but obviously, it was prey for minority groups and one had to keep an eye upon it.

From almost day one, because I tended to compare it with the Chichester R.D.C. and the West Sussex County Council - both admirably run local authorities, Bognor left a lot to be desired. To give an example - a house was to be built next door to our own at Craigwell; naturally we were concerned as to what was going to be built there, so I asked - at the public desk - for a sight of the plans. I was refused. I then got stroppy and pointed out my statutory rights as a ratepayer and voter in the town, to see the plans. When I demanded this in such terms, they were produced immediately - but I naturally thought of other ratepayers who might not have known in similar circumstances it was their statutory right. Some time later, I told the then deputy clerk what had happened - and he said, in effect, whatever councillors asked for, "my practice is to give them what they want." The point about it being a statutory right for *everyone* to see and instructing his staff accordingly, being completely ignored.

In the Conservative Party - we have/had a tradition that meetings should not ordinarily last longer than 1½ hours (obviously subject to special cases). I recall in my short time on the urban council, by the absence of the committee chairman, I was invited as vice-chairman to take the chair. We were getting along famously, on about item 5, a former council chairman said that I was going too fast, we should revisit item 3 (which had already been passed). After that, I gave up over Bognor - in local government terms, it seemed that Bognor was not as other places, and the ordinary rules of debate did not apply. But that did not mean it was corrupt.

But before the time came for me to stand down, Bognor Regis U.D.C. erupted in the most extraordinary fashion - see Appendix II.

* * * * *

Myself receiving Lord Hailsham at Stationers' Hall on the occasion of the 150th Anniversary of the "Justice of the Peace", with Lady Hailsham and Mrs Barry Rose in the background.

When Lord Hailsham as Lord Chancellor, came as our guest to the 150th anniversary dinner to mark the founding of the *Justice of the Peace*, we soon found we were speaking about the Suez Campaign. He had been First Lord of the Admiralty at the time, and he was quite emotional about the possibility of our men who had been killed in battle being dismembered and defiled by the Egyptians - and how it had been essential for their bodies to be recovered, even at the cost of further casualties.

He had had some terrible disappointments and much sadness in his personal life - the major one, I imagine, was the loss of his second wife in a riding accident while they were both on holiday in Australia. There are those who have remarked upon his uncertain temperament; however, speaking personally, I always found him courteous and polite, even although I suspect that sometimes we would meet in unexpected places, and he would not know who I was. If we met in the street, for example, we would each doff our bowlers at the other; today, it seems a different world entirely.

* * * * *

About a year later I entertained Lord Mackay, the new Lord Chancellor, who in the interim had replaced Lord Havers, who in turn had replaced Hailsham, at a dinner to mark the 150th Anniversary of the founding of *Justice of the Peace Reports*. Lord Mackay told me how he became Lord Chancellor - he was asked to go to No.10 and Mrs. Thatcher, as she then was, asked him whether he would accept. He said, "I'll have to ask my wife first." Mrs. Thatcher motioned towards a telephone and said, "Go ahead." His wife was out shopping, and it was about an hour and a half later before she returned, and he was able to give an affirmative answer to the Prime Minister. Thus are the great Offices of State decided!

I have known so many Lord Chancellors (not, of course, at such close quarters, because we had run out of 150 year-old anniversary celebrations!) since the war - and with just one exception, I have found all to have been delightful people.

* * * * *

Once upon a time, I had the dream of being a novelist/playwright - but alas, like many of my dreams - apart from a few published short stories, this particular dream came to naught, and when I was about 30, as I was getting nowhere and was in a mood of some depression, I gathered together all the manuscripts I could find, and used the garden incinerator. But what I had forgotten was my long-suffering literary agent, and some years later (obviously, after he had retired) his successor duly sent me five or six of my novels, which he said he had found in a cupboard. They were all dog-eared, showing they had been doing the rounds of the publishers, so I do not regard their find as being a 'literary sensation'. With possibly one exception, they too deserved the incinerator.

But ... it had been on the coldest night (up to then) of the century, so anyone with any sense would not have expected the critics to have turned up on such a night for a new play by an unknown author, and they didn't. But in this try-out theatre in the West End, there were eight or nine curtain calls and I remember thinking that it had been a success - but of course the humiliation of being ignored (except for a meaningless notice in *The Stage)* meant I thought no more about it.

And then ... years later, a friend of my sister's on holiday in Africa arrived in Bulawayo, and went to the local playhouse, and she wrote my sister more or less on these lines: "We went to the local theatre last night and saw a play by Barry Rose called 'Funny Business'. Any relation?"

Well, in the way these things are done, copies of the play had been sent to New York, Sydney and Cape Town and obviously the Cape Town connection had been responsible for the staging - years later - in Bulawayo - of the play, but needless to say I received no royalties, and somehow I do not think I ever will. But bearing in mind the mess our then Colonial Office made of those bits of Africa coloured red on the old atlases, and especially that part of Zimbabwe containing Bulawayo where ethnic/tribal murder has been on an horrific scale, if my play brought just a little lightness, they are very welcome.

But nevertheless, what a coincidence.

H.B. Wilson, a friend at the Home Office, was late in arriving for luncheon. In apologising, he said, "You'll never guess what I have been doing this morning - I have been at Brixton Prison, 6 a.m., supervising the exhumation of the remains of Roger Casement for them to be sent via Heathrow to the Republic of Ireland where apparently, for some, he is regarded almost as a saint." It will be remembered Casement was a diplomat in the British Foreign Office, and he had a predilection for little boys. His dairies detailed his exploits in this field (in various South American countries) - they were called "The Black Diaries" and after his conviction as a traitor for his part in trying to raise armed rebellion in Ireland, while the Great War was being waged in all its ferocity. In U.S.A. public opinion was said to be in sympathy with Casement, and the Black Diaries (naturally) were alleged by the IRA and its friends, to be forgeries.

I asked Wilson - why had we found it necessary to execute Casement? Why did we not treat him as a joke (for his whole part in the Rebellion was organized quite absurdly) - but Wilson, with access to all the private files of the period, said that the feeling in the U.K. (including Ireland which at the time was still, wholly, part of the UK and - then - generally sympathetic to the cause of the Allies) was so strong and so bitter that there was no alternative to his execution. The Black Diaries were used in the Embassies in the U.S. and elsewhere to show the chap was in every respect a Bad Egg.

* * * * *

I met a member of a law firm in New York, which had had as one of its partners Mr. Thomas Dewey as Presidential Candidate. (It will be remembered he had been State Prosecutor for New York

State.)

The battle between him and his Democratic opponent had been a fierce one, and as seems so often the case in American Presidential Elections, there were allegations of jiggery-pokery during the election and during the count. Indeed, I fancy Dewey had been the subject of screaming headlines saying he had won, whereas he had lost. It must have been very disappointing for him. Anyway, after the Election, he paid a visit to the offices of his law firm, and members of that firm, as he prepared to go upstairs, so perhaps sarcastically or ironically, sang "Hail the Chief" which I gather is some sort of patriotic anthem in honour of the President.

He never visited his old firm again, according to my informant.

* * * * *

I am in this book mainly concerned with spontaneous speech, but I think there must be room for the occasional departure from the rule. The following is an extract from correspondence received. Professor Lee Sheridan, a barrister who has never practised as such, and instead has had a rather adventurous academic life. Few academics, I imagine, can have served in Belfast, Malaya (where a whole volume was dedicated by others to his academic achievements in that country), and Cardiff University (which was at one time so strapped for cash, he had to run two departments at once). He and I have exchanged letters since the days when he first came into my sights as one of the editors of *Anglo-American Law Review*, (he now lives in Wales) and the following gives a flavour of his wit:

"You are mistaken in thinking that, in order to enter Wales, you must be in possession of a Visa. Barclaycard or American Express will do, or even coins provided they are made in Wales.

"I admit that I have a problem about raising the entry tax, which is now some considerable number of pence in excess of four pounds; but such is the magnetism of the Principality that most Englishmen get into their cars for the sole purpose of queueing up to pay it. Crossing from Wales to England being free, statisticians have noticed that the eastbound carriageway of the Severn bridges are busier than the westbound and have concluded that Wales is being steadily depopulated. You would of course evade the tolls by getting on a train and, if Railtrack were having a good day, you might reach your destination or at least someone's.

"There is a strong case for Englishmen to leave a country where they cannot afford to live. From time to time I consider moving, but careful perusal of *The Times* shows that no English house I could bear to live in costs less than fifteen million pounds whereas a mansion in Glyncorrwg can be had for forty thousand. And we have an Assembly. I note with pleasure that sixty per cent of the population of the Principality joined me in abstaining as our indication of disapproval of the Assembly's existence. We pray that enough people will stay in England to pay for it as we should not relish doing so ourselves."

APPENDIX I:

I had occasion (on the business of the Association of Councillors) to go with Gerry Reynolds (who was then Minister for War) to see the then Minister for Housing and Local Government. The purpose of that meeting is now immaterial - but it was shortly after the Bognor Regis U.D.C. had dismissed its Clerk (or, as he was wont to call himself, "The Town Clerk") and there had been an Inquiry. As I left the room - Gerry, having other business to transact, stayed. He told me subsequently that the Minister had said to him, as I was walking out of the room, "there goes the man who saved Bognor Regis."

Well, that was nice of him - and truly, I think there was some truth in it.

It was in fact an episode which I believe was unique in 20th century Local Government. As I have recounted here, when going to London, and indeed elsewhere, one heard the most outrageous slanders committed against various Councillors of the Bognor Regis U.D.C. and as chairman of the Conservative Association for the Constituency (with Bognor as its largest constituent part) I was concerned for the interests of the Conservative Party as well as for the town. Were the individuals collectively or individually corrupt? I said to John Pitt, the then Agent, that I would become a member and find out for myself what was going on; he was horrified as he already thought I had more than enough to do. I got myself elected, and soon formed the opinion (I am a former member of the Royal Institute for Public Administration) that in terms of efficiency it was lacking, with meetings which went on interminably and with agendas disregarded - but of corruption? Of course not - just ordinary decent people trying to do something for the town in which they lived, and possibly to escape the boredom of being retired.

So anyway, having satisfied myself on this matter, I informed my branch which had selected me that they had to look out for another candidate.

But a new Clerk was appointed, who soon made no bones about going on television and in effect of accusing his councillors (or some of them) of voting on matters in which they had a pecuniary interest - almost corruption. The local press and television certainly did not help, and in the end, an eminent Queen's Counsel (Mr. Ramsay Willis) (from local government chambers) just about to be appointed a High Court Judge, came to Bognor to hold an inquiry into the whole business which ultimately had involved the dismissal of the clerk.

When I say that at one stage, the Town Clerk of Southampton, the Author of "The Law of Elections" and someone of immense Local Government experience, said that if Bognor U.D.C. did not sack Mr. Smith quickly he'd come over and do it himself, it gives some idea of the situation; the Society of Clerks of U.D.C.s expressed their support for the Council's action - the Society being in existence to protect, *inter alia*, the interests of Clerks.

As for myself, Mr. Smith's solicitors duly warned me. They were to issue a writ for libel.

For myself I submitted a memorandum of 144 pages for the edification of Mr. Ramsay Willis (I remember saying to Tom Hayward, the then Clerk of the West Sussex County Council, that I had done this, when we were in the 'men's room' at County Hall. I recall he said I should be ashamed of myself. It was said only partly in jest - he was concerned with the good name of local government in the county. And of course he at that stage had no idea of the ramifications of the matter. Subsequently I was to ask him to be prepared to 'loan' us one of his assistant solicitors, for we were not to know whether - at that particular stage, the Deputy Clerk, Mr. Richard Sheppard, would stay on and we wanted to be sure that Bognor would be properly administered when the Report was published.

But still, it was all a very remarkable business - when I am dead, my report was (and I have re-read it now) a remarkable document of this most extraordinary of local matters. It is the sort of thing that would make television dramas or a film or a novel. But there goes the man who saved Bognor Regis 'according' to the Minister, a remark probably resulting from the Minister himself having read my report. I suspect it would have made a change from the diet normally served up for Ministers. And it all began in consequence of the slanders I heard said on the train previously and decided in consequence to dip my toe in the Bognor waters. The role of the local press, etc., I give in the following Appendix. I have lodged a copy of my observations - all 144 pages of them - with the County Archives to await a decent period after my demise. The flavour of what happened will be found in Appendix II, *post.*

APPENDIX II:

Although the following letter was written by Barry Rose and signed by all Conservative members of the Bognor Regis U.D.C. - by the time it was sent he was no longer a member of the Council himself and Charles Youngman had been elected Leader of the Conservatives on the U.D.C. However, he did not favour Barry Rose with a copy of the reply that Sir Samuel Storey sent, saying that it was only the usual sort of guff that one would expect. From this I gathered it was no sort of reply at all. Bill Loveys - at that time Bognor's M.P. - told me that Sam Storey had sought him out in the House and said he had received the letter - "I said to him that if Barry Rose had anything to do with it, you can bet it was right." I mention this merely because I cannot produce the letter he sent in reply to what follows. Nevertheless, I would have liked to have seen it. I doubt if Sir Sam had anything to do with it - as in Who's Who he did not even mention his connection with Portsmouth and Sunderland Newspapers.

Letter composed by Barry Rose and signed by all Conservative Members of the Bognor Regis U.D.C., and sent to the Chairman of Portsmouth and Sunderland Newspapers Ltd., (Sir Samuel Story, Bart., M.P. (Con.), (and subsequently Baron Buckton, life peer) Chairman of Portsmouth and Sunderland Newspapers Ltd., publishers inter alia, of the Bognor Regis Observer. The letter that follows was not used by the Bognor Regis Observer at the time. Of course, it was not addressed to the Editor - but I would be surprised indeed if it was not sent to the Editor for comment, if not explanation.

Bognor Regis is predominately a Conservative town. Eleven of the 18 councillors are Conservative; three additional councillors are supported (as independents) by a local Conservative Branch Association. The Conservative Parliamentary majority for the constituency as a whole is one of the largest in the country.

We do not expect the local Press to be always Conservative in tone just because the majority of the townspeople evidentially think as well as vote Conservative. What we have always had in the past, however, is fair reporting - that is to say, we have had a fair allocation of space, or at least, not noticeably less space than you give to other parties. However, this does not seem to have been the case just recently.

It is our wish to be on friendly terms with the local press, not because we want any favours from them, but because we realise that they are here to serve the public just as in our own sphere, so are we. The politics of your individual reporters are none of our business, and you may say that how you run your newspapers is also none of our business. Of course it is not, but the whole purpose of our wishing to have an interview with you is to ascertain from you that you in fact realise just how far your *Bognor Regis Observer* seems to have departed from its previous fairness, and to ask for a return to that fairness.

We in Bognor Regis have been confronted for 12 months with a position of unprecedented difficulty in local government. The good faith of our members has been attacked again and again, but whereas we expect the national press to use whatever dirt they can against people in public life (and Bognor Regis councillors are fair game in this respect), the local press must surely be different, as in a sense, in a small town such as this, we are all members of the same family.

Basically, the problem has been one of *Council v. Clerk*. It so happens that the Council is Conservative - the former clerk is

Liberal (he is now a Liberal parliamentary candidate) - although to say the matter is purely political is however, an over-simplification. Most of our members, if not actually born in Bognor, have certainly spent the majority of their lives in the town - they have served other Associations, done other public work, possibly been engaged in business in the town for years, before they were elected to the Council. In other words, they have known the town for years, and to be nominated under the Conservative label, they have to satisfy Conservative Branch Committees as to their integrity when they stood for election and were elected.

The 11 elected Conservative members must have been between them accumulated public service to the town in one capacity or another, amounting, literally, in a cumulative sense, to hundreds of years. Yet within months of the arrival of the new Clerk, all this was put at naught.

If you will refer to your files for December last, you will see the Clerk is there reported as warning the Councillors against their infringement of Section 76 of the Local Government Act 1933. In the same issue you publish a leading article. Your placard for the week's issue included the item - "Clerk Warns Councillors". Nothing could have been more harmful to our Councillor members than this, as destroying public confidence in them. Had this been a "normal" warning, you may speculate as to why the Clerk did not warn his employers (the Council) in private. However, the "warning" was made in public, and we certainly would not criticise your publication of this item, or your comment, or your placard. What we do criticise is that not one of our members was asked for comment on a subject which had been sprung upon them in open Council, without their prior knowledge or consent, although it was not sprung upon your reporters, who had been given a press release beforehand by the Clerk.

By itself, this item may be thought unworthy of mention - all right, a mistake is made; everyone makes mistakes - do not make a fuss. It is mentioned here, however, for each story has to start somewhere, and this was indeed the start of the whole campaign.

Frequently, various members of the local press (not just your own reporters) were to be seen leaving the Clerk's office, doubtless after confidential "chats" with the Clerk. What was said, naturally we do not know, but it seems to us that as a result of these confidential chats, various members of the Council on the Conservative side, who previously had been on friendly terms with your reporters almost as long as your reporters had been in Bognor, were now regarded by them (your staff) with the utmost reserve, if not indeed with suspicion.

We do not know what was said about our members in these private chats - although we can guess its nature from what has been subsequently published. We are not concerned with this aspect of it at all - if your reporters are invited to attend private meetings by the Clerk for "background", of course they would attend and listen to what was said, although naturally we would have wished that they had asked us privately, and "off the record" just what was going on. After all, they had known us long enough, we would have thought, to have asked this without in any way compromising their own position as journalists. We could not institute this, as we ourselves did not know in the early days (when the seeds were being sown for what was to happen subsequently) what was going on, on the other side. This however is not in any way a complaint; rather is it a regret. It is, however, germane to the fundamental issue.

You will appreciate that we do not possess copies of all newspapers published since this dispute began, but on those we still have, the following is based:

On January 27, 1965, the Evening News (the reporters are

apparently the same as for the Observer - and we have noticed that the stories are sometimes used in the Observer from the News) reported an "angry Council reaction" to a television news item attributed to the Clerk, that the town's redevelopment project was postponed, with a denial of this by the appropriate committee chairman. The Clerk denied he had ever given a statement about it. (The television "contact" locally is apparently Mr. Williams, who is responsible for your 'Belinda' column). The Observer for February 2nd has a leading article commenting on the Council's "disturbing lack of confidence in, and contact with, the Council by its townspeople," and commending the Clerk's habit of holding monthly press conferences. As for the "disturbing lack of confidence," the Conservatives and their supporters won every seat (in some cases with increased majorities) they contested in May. Already, however, it was obvious that the line-up of *Council v. Clerk* was taking place in your columns, with the Clerk receiving editorial support.

In the issue of March 26th of the Observer, the affair begins to get under way. Here we see Mr. Smith announcing a "police probe" - the announcement not coming from the police, but from Mr. Smith, and also from Mr. Campion (who, even by then, was the Council's No. 1 critic - if this be not an understatement). Nothing could be more calculated to inspire lack of confidence in the Council than this. Naturally, we do not criticise the Observer for printing this, but although your reporter evidently asked the opinion of the police (who would not comment) and the Vicar of Bognor (who said he had asked all churches to pray for Chairman, Clerk and Council), again, no one on the Council was asked to comment. Although we had no warning of this announcement, we understand your reporters did.

Next we come to the issue of April 2nd, where you will see the headline "Bognor Council - Inquiry Likely". Here, an item of news is given an anti-Council slant; you will see that the Clerk is fully quoted - Mr. Campion is also quoted - but no one from the Council is apparently even invited to speak, although it was supposed to be the Council ordering the Inquiry. If you look at this item, you will see no hint given that a Council cannot dismiss its servant; you will see the Clerk mis-stated facts (for the Minister has no power to order an Inquiry, let alone carry one out), but you will not see any comment requested from a Conservative Councillor. In the same issue, you have, "C.I.D. Probe - Liberals' Statement", also containing a statement from a Conservative who at that time was clearly a renegade from the Conservative Group, as well as a further statement by Mr. Smith, describing what had been a perfectly proper meeting in the Chairman of the Council's house as a "clandestine" one. No word from the Council is used. As for the Inquiry, it is true that the Council subsequently - four months subsequently, and after quite unprecedented pressure from, amongst others, your own newspapers - asked for one, but the headline and the story clearly, at that stage, indicated that the Council was in the wrong, thus mixing news and comment as one.

In the issue for April 9th, in a leading article, after being savagely critical of the Council's record (which was fair comment in a column of comment), you will see, "Now the Minister of Housing etc. is to be asked to conduct an Inquiry into the administration and conduct of the Urban Council." The Minister was being asked to do no such thing; at that stage, he was being asked to advise upon the holding of an Inquiry, and in any case he has no power to conduct an Inquiry of this sort.

You publish a letter in this issue from Mr. Downer (subsequently to be closely identified as a close supporter of the Clerk), on the subject of an article written in another newspaper entirely, by the Divisional Conservative Chairman, Mr. Barry Rose. Mr. Rose considered his views had been wrongly represented in a newspaper whose readers, for the most part (as the correspondence in the Observer is used in all editions away from Bognor), could have no means of reading what he had actually said. He therefore replied in your issue of May 7th. A further letter from Mr. Downer, containing the most extravagant criticism of Mr. Rose and his previous article published elsewhere, under the heading of "Tactics that are to be Deplored," is published in the issue for May 21st, with the footnote that the editor regrets that the correspondence must now end.

In the issue for May 14th, it is reported that the Clerk is accused of suppressing information by the Council. Whereas, whenever the Council was under attack, no one was ever asked to reply (see above), here we see Mr. Smith reported in the same issue saying the Council is speaking absolute nonsense. In other words, *he* had been asked.

In your issue of May 21st, your headline reads, "Mr. Smith is in the Clear" - not, it will be noted - "Mr. Smith says he is in the Clear". But again, comment is quite in abundance from Mr. Smith - you will look in vain for comment invited from the Council.

In the same issue, there is a leading article saying that Mr. Smith "had not been approached to give an explanation prior to the meeting". In view of the criticisms published in the Observer with no approach by the Observer to the Council for any explanation, you may think this comment is indicative.

Now we come to the Evening News of May 15th. Here we see as your headline story the summonsing of a Conservative Councillor for what was - at worst - a technical offence of the most minor nature imaginable, which subsequently resulted in an absolute discharge, and even on this, is now the subject of an Appeal to the

High Court. Can this alleged offence really have warranted this amount of publicity? If it did, it shows pretty clearly how the affair had been blown up through the type of publicity we have already criticised.

Against this sort of background, the Conservative Councillors won the local government elections (see your issue of May 21st). To have won despite the incredible campaign of innuendo that had been carried on against them, of which the above are some of the samples, was itself a remarkable achievement, as the whole campaign had been fought on the integrity of the Council. It was a truly dirty campaign that was waged against us. Yet your headline is, "Election Result was in line with national trend".

In the issue of May 28th is the story, "Council Peace Move by Minister", where again comment is interpolated into a news story. For example, in the third paragraph, it is said, "Mr. Smith subsequently refuted these accusations with the aid of a letter from the Ministry". Seven Councillors, including even a Liberal, had signed the report on what they had been told at the Ministry - they may have been wrong, they may have been right - but in the previous sentence the word "allegedly" is applied to their findings; the definitive "refuted" is applied to Mr. Smith's.

In the same issue, it will be seen that, "Mr. Smith Alleges 'Threats'". This is a very serious innuendo; so far as we know, you asked for no comment on it at all.

Very naturally, the Observer reports - in the issue of June 4th - with much publicity - the scenes which occurred following the dismissal of the Clerk. You give prominence to the observations of the Liberals - although they were in a 3-12 minority - we accept that the Conservatives at this meeting said virtually nothing, for they had said their piece at an earlier meeting when the press were excluded. Your newspaper reports, however, Mr. Smith's observations on, "When I began my drive to improve the Public Service in Bognor," but no one on our side was asked what they thought of this; neither - to our knowledge - was the former Clerk (Mr. Hill), who had served as Clerk for 25 years prior to Mr. Smith, and therefore, one might think, in a reasonably good position to state what, if anything, was wrong with the Bognor Council - asked to comment.

After the dismissal, the Observer gave much space to the efforts of various of Mr. Smith's friends, such as his former landlady (—) - although not stating it was his former landlady - to get an Inquiry into the dismissal. Not one of our Conservative members was asked for an off-the-record chat, or for a formal interview. People such as Mr. White (Evening News, May 31st) are quoted as saying that there was feeling in the town because Mr. Smith was, "dismissed in an undemocratic manner at a private meeting of the Council". Your issue of Evening News, May 28th, shows just how private that meeting was.

On July 2nd, the Observer reports, "Mr. Smith's Campaign to clean up Local Government continues. EX-CLERK LAUNCHES A LAW REFORM SOCIETY". It is reported that Mr. Smith had launched his Society in London the previous Tuesday. London is a large place - the report does not state what part of London, or who attended the meeting, apart from Mr. Smith. (This had some relevance as only last weekend - November 6th - it was nationally reported that the first formal meeting of Mr. Smith's Society was held). Throughout, the Observer pressed the Council to give all details to the public - but it seems to be the case that Mr. Smith is subject to different considerations. The aims of the Society are given, but not for example, that Bognor Council already admits the press to committee meetings. No Conservative is asked for comments on this, although the story is plainly angled against the

Council. In the same issue, there is a "resign" call to the U.D.C. by the newly-formed so-called Civic Protection Society. Frequent publicity is given to this body (say 300 members), but the Conservative Branch Association has a membership of about 5,000 for the town. Mrs. Thorne, a member of the Liberal Executive, begins to get her quota of publicity at this stage. She is interviewed, and the headline is, "District Auditor told of Alleged Waste", but the Treasurer of the Council is not approached at all for his comments. It goes without saying that the Conservative Chairman of the Finance Committee was not asked either, or any Conservative member.

In your issue of July 9th, you have a leading article generally in favour of the B.B.C. programme dealing with Bognor. That 2 Liberals appeared on that programme; that only 1 Conservative councillor was asked, but 10 Conservative councillors were not, shows pretty clearly how this programme was weighted - your writer did not ask us our opinion as to whether it was fair or whether the B.B.C. was, in our opinion, right in what it claimed.

In your issue of August 13th, here the apparent bias comes out in the highly selective "diary" of events as printed. The "diary" starts off with March 23rd, with the allegation of a "Star Chamber", but had whoever was responsible gone back earlier in his back copies, he might have seen why there had to be this meeting in the first place. After March 23rd, we see under April 27th a deputation being sent to Whitehall does not include the fact that at this Council Meeting Mr. Smith had not reported to the Council he had heard from the Ministry and that this information was obtained from an independent source - relevant, one would think, in relation to the entry for May 11th. Under May 18th, Mr. Smith is said to have refuted a charge of suppressing information as given in the item shown under May 11th. Under June 4th, it is said that Bognor

NALGO expressed its grave concern at the dismissal of Mr. Smith. (NALGO has informed us that they asked for a correction for the original item, which was never forthcoming). Then we see under June 27th, Mr. Smith's Society to Clean Up Local Government (see above) is noted.

Significantly, the Chairman of the Council's statement that an earlier statement expressing confidence in the Clerk had been written by the Clerk himself, is not mentioned. A statement by a Conservative Councillor (Mr. Goldsmith) releasing the text of a letter he had received from Mr. Smith telling him that Mr. Smith was proceeding with legal action against another councillor, and if other councillors said anything, it would make matters worse for the member concerned, is also ignored. Correspondence released by the Vice-Chairman of the Council (Mr. Vincent), making a nonsense of Mr. Smith's printed observations on tendering by Councillors, was also ignored. One would have thought in a "diary" purporting to [be] matters leading up to the dismissal of the Clerk, which in turn led up to the Inquiry, that these were highly relevant matters.

In your issue of October 1st, your Observer has, "Ex-Clerk hits out at Council". By now evidently the bias is beginning to wear off, as this time the Chairman of an appropriate Council committee is invited to give his comments.

If you would like further examples, these can be supplied. If you start reading your "Belinda" column this year, you will see examples practically every week of the sort of thing which is the subject of this, and if you like, we will specify particular items, even although most issues of the Observer are no longer available for us as they have been destroyed. Here, however, we have no comment to make - those items are "gossip" rather than straight news.

Another aspect of the matter has been some of the items which have not been published. We could provide many examples where in our opinion, items favourable to ourselves have been omitted. Here, however, we recognise that we are on more unsure ground, for you have always considerations of available space to consider, and we cannot, and do not, seriously take exception to the reports as published of Council meetings, etc., where in the published version you may have left out items that we may consider to be highly relevant points in our defence over all the attacks made upon us.

It is, however, on the grounds of an item being omitted that we finally decided to take the matter up with you. Whilst we recognise your space difficulties, and ordinarily would not complain about the omission of any particular item, there was an item which in our view should have been published on its essential news value. In your issue of October 22nd, you publish a statement by the Chairman of the Conservative Association on the role of the Liberals in the whole dispute. Another local paper printed the same story, but asked the Liberals for their comments; in doing so they brought in the local M.P. (Mr. Loveys). Mr. Loveys stated that the Liberals' statement was untrue, insofar as it related to him. On any basis, this was worthy of inclusion, as a news item. It is true that the original Liberal statement was in another local newspaper, not your own, but this had not stopped the Observer from printing a letter (or letters) attacking the Chairman of the Conservative Party for Chichester, on the basis of what had appeared in the other newspaper. It was, in our view, the culmination of the partiality in reporting of the Observer. Incidentally, the same issue contains a "puff" in its "diary" feature for a forthcoming Liberal event - although we have been told that the Observer never gives future publicity to a forthcoming event (presumably so that we should take paid advertising space to do so).

We wanted to discuss these matters with you privately, through the Leader of the Conservative Group, as we do not wish to make trouble between ourselves and your staff who are stationed in Bognor. Your insistence, however, that we should give you details, has resulted in our going into more detail than otherwise would have been the case. We know that circumstances have been completely exceptional in Bognor. When matters were at their height, and when we considered we were being badly used by your newspapers, we did not complain then. But we consider it is essential, now that the Inquiry is over, that the Council should be able to get on with its work in a reasonable sort of atmosphere. Your newspapers can continue to attack us whenever they consider we do wrong, and we did not have the slightest objection to this. It can continue to be as Liberal-flavoured as you like; it is your newspaper and you will do what you please with it. We are not making any complaint; we are merely asking whether you are aware how very biased the Observer has recently become.

Conservative Group Leader   Vice-Chairman of the Council

All signatures are those   Chairman,
of Members of the Council   Chichester Conservative Association

Liberal report

Quite by chance came into my hands the press release relating to the annual 'report' of the Association of Liberal Councillors, presented by its chairman, Alderman David Evans. The report included the following passage:

"The handling of the Bognor Regis affair provides an excellent example of successful co-operation. Headquarters were advised of the position by the two Liberal councillors at Bognor. Members of the A.L.C. [Association of Liberal Councillors] standing Committee met Paul Smith, the dismissed Town Clerk (sic).

A plan of action was formulated. Professor Brian Keith-Lucas, chairman of the Liberal Party's 1962 Local Government Committee, was consulted. A Press conference was held and a resolution was placed before the Party Council.

The result - widespread publicity. We need more of this type of co-operation between local councillors, the A.L.C., and headquarters. Allying a campaign to a particular instance produces the best results."

It seemed, somehow, a fitting conclusion. I know that I would never have known the depth of the involvement of the Liberal Councillors in this sad and sorrowful affair had not the above come into my hands for possible inclusion in the *Local Government Review*, a national local government journal which I used to publish. I would never have dreamt that honourable people could have deliberately got themselves involved in this appalling business - involving their fellow councillors in wasted personal expenditure of hundreds of pounds in legal costs in addition to their personal worry, with one councillor being taken to hospital with a slit wrist (apparently, had his next door neighbour not been a nurse and at home, he would have died).

So far as I know, not one word of apology or regret or explanation has been offered by them.

APPENDIX III:

Background to letter <u>not</u> sent to Chief Executive of West Sussex County Council

The following letter was written in June 1989. I believe the 'Brief History' to which it refers was published some time before and I knew about it only then as a result of my attention being drawn to it.

I had always an agreeable and friendly relationship with John Hooley, the Chief Executive, and I did not want to risk impairing that relationship, even although by this time I was 'off' the County Council. As a result, the letter was never sent. Yet in the course of preparation of this book, I came across it again. On reflection, and at this remove in time, John Hooley (who is now retired) might be amused rather than otherwise. I certainly hope so. And also, dare I say it, its historical content might be of interest for others writing books on the history of local government, in the County. Of course, John Hooley himself would never have been involved in the wording of "The First Hundred Years". However, at the time it was published, he <u>was</u> Chief Executive, and would have shouldered the responsibility for it, subject of course, to the very ultimate responsibility of the Council itself. (He probably will be bemused at the reference to Jeffrey Archer - for I have left the letter as I originally wrote it - warts and all!) As it happens, I think it rather ties in with my letter to David Blacker, post.

John Hooley Esq
Chief Executive
West Sussex County Council
County Hall
Chichester

> **LETTER NOT SENT**

21st June 1989

Dear John

West Sussex County Council
The First 100 Years

I have expended some of my hard-earned money on the purchase of the above, and feel that really I should write you about it on a number of counts.

First, the very fact that it is being claimed to be the 'first 100 years'. The county council which came into existence in 1889 as a result of the Act of 1888, was ended by the Act of 1972. As the compilers of the publication plainly refuse to accept the word of an Act of Parliament, there is always Halsbury, which at vol.28, para.1008, says, "The county, county borough, non-county borough, rural district and urban parish councils in England and Wales, which were existing on 31st March 1974, ceased to exist, that is, were abolished on 1st April, 1974." Succinct, and to the point. I do not think the Act of Parliament completely escaped the notice of West Sussex County Council, for I seem to remember being told of a rather mournful occasion at County Hall being held on 31st March 1974 to mark its demise.

Therefore, in the sense that 'the first 100 years' infers a continuous period, it is plainly at fault. The fact that many other county councils have published their own equally spurious histories (spurious, that is, when related to the term 'centenary') is neither here not there. The secondary fact that the Association of County Councils (the natural successor to the former County Councils' Association) has lent itself to this deception and has conned Her Majesty the Queen into attending a function in celebration thereof, again is neither here nor there, but everyone involved in the deception can reflect upon what would have been their fate in earlier times!

The short answer is that local government has been continuous in the country for many centuries, and taking many different forms; the latest county council (*post* 1972 Act model) carries on the tradition but that is manifestly not the same, and was indeed specifically said by Parliament not to be the same, as its predecessor council. A constitutional lawyer could argue that by lending Herself to the deception, in attending the reception given by the A.C.C., the Queen Herself was acting unconstitutionally as against the expressed will of Parliament. But I am sure that all of you are far too nice to end up in the Tower.

Secondly, the work - by prolific use of illustrations - looks handsome, but sadly, in my opinion, its appearance is not matched by the accompanying text. For example, the reference to Clerks of the Peace, the phrase (p.12) that "the first Clerks of the Peace must have been (sic) appointed in the 14th century". Bearing in mind that the Society of Clerks of the Peace published an invaluable reference book as a grand farewell gesture to the world they were required to leave, which gave the name of every Clerk of the Peace who had been appointed from inception, which I have and which I have little doubt the compilers of the publication have or could have found easy access to, the use of such a phrase as 'must have been appointed' is slovenly and certainly not one to be expected in a work where the then Chairman in his foreword specifically mentions 'value for money' in the context of the work. In the 'Early Beginnings' it says 'Quarter Sessions ... were given powers to levy a rate'. No mention of statute labour, which if the work is dealing with the subject seriously and speaking truly of 'Early Beginnings', would surely have deserved some mention because of its importance in a county context especially. There are other omissions: for example, a photograph of the first chief constable of West Sussex appears on p.14 - but nothing is said of the last, and how he came to be the last.

I accept, of course, that there has to be an element of selection of what appears and what does not and it must always be a matter of opinion as to what is and what is not published. My own opinion is that the title and the imprint should give an indication, and in my view the book is not a proper history but an illustrated guide which certainly is inadequate and in some areas positively misleading, possibly more suitable as a free gift to very young children rather than being put on sale at nearly £6. We do not, after all, want to involve your Trading Standards Department!

But these are intended as rather light-hearted comments compared to what I now have to say. I regard as serious the reference to me on p.85. To begin with, the publication speaks of me as being 'of Chichester'. I represented North Mundham and Aldingbourne respectively, but never Chichester, and I have never lived in the city. It speaks of 'first attempts' by me to organise a Conservative group. No such attempts by me were ever made. I recall attempts by others in the 1950s and 1960s to establish a Conservative Group, but I was involved with no attempt, although I did attend one of the (very poorly attended) meetings.

What I was associated with was certainly not organised or called by me or by any other member of the council. At the behest of the then Chairman of the Conservative Party, Edward du Cann, the constituency associations in West Sussex organised a meeting which took place in an hotel in Worthing, which was chaired by the then chairman of the Party's National Local Government Advisory Committee (Arthur Jones, M.P.), and if there was an organiser as such at all, it was the National Secretary to that Advisory Committee. As a result of that meeting, on that very evening the Group came into being, with 44 members paying their subscriptions (two were subsequently to resign, although later they resumed their membership), and later that evening (with Arthur Jones still in the chair) officers were elected, and I became the first Leader. Can this really be called an 'attempt'? Subsequently, the membership was increased to 79 (out of a total membership of 96) when the Independents who had for the most part stood with Conservative support, joined en bloc, thus giving it the largest majority of any Conservative Group in England, with all the problems attendant upon such a huge majority. I will not speak of these difficulties, but I can speak of the unstinting admiration

I certainly had which I am sure was shared by my friends, for the Leader of the Opposition, who of course was not a member at all, but who was able to even things up very considerably. It was to cope with this and the situation of an excessively large majority that I formed a group within a group (not the Committee) of which Christopher Buckle was never invited to be a member (by my recollection, I do not think he was ever a member of the Group's Committee, either).

When after five years I decided not to stand for re-election, our 'group within a group' invited [at my suggestion] Christopher Buckle to a meeting in my office in Chichester to take over from me or rather, to accept nomination - but in practical politics it amounted to the same thing. He was duly elected by the Group at its next annual general meeting. Why we selected him is something your compilers could not be expected to know, and for the matter of that, I suppose that even now Christopher Buckle does not know, either. But this is by the way. [This 'group within a group' was founded - if it is of any interest at this remove in time - following personal invitations extended by me to certain individual members in whom I had every confidence; likewise, I take the responsibility of suggesting Buckle as my successor.]

I certainly did not ask or expect any mention of the Group's beginnings in the predecessor Council to be made, or of myself, but I would most definitely expect that if any mention is to be made by the successor council, at least it should be accurate. If it is made, it should not be demeaning to the extent of denying the existence of something which manifestly was in existence, and the slighting reference to myself not only being inaccurate but also plainly actionable as bringing what was achieved and the reference to me personally, into contempt, if not ridicule. After Koo Stark, Jeffrey Archer and Mrs. Sutcliffe - who knows what vast fortune awaits me in the High Court? It is also insulting in the sense that it is contemptuous of my colleagues, many of whom, alas, are now dead, and who worked so hard to establish the Group which the publication now so airily dismisses, and of which I am pretty sure the present Group and the present County Council was able to benefit from - if only from the past chairmanships of Christopher Buckle and Peter Sheppard.

You, I am sure, had it drummed into you when studying law - check your references. If people are writing about contemporary, or nearly contemporary, history, it is surely doubly important that they should check their references, for whereas the dead have no means of redress, those who are still alive, have. The whole paragraph, insofar as it relates to me, is plainly actionable. What are you going to do about it?

I suggest for a beginning that it is about time you had luncheon with me.

Yours ever

Barry Rose

APPENDIX IV:

Letter to David Blacker Esq, former member of the County Council for East Ward, Chichester

Dear David   5 November 1991

Many years have passed since we last met - that occasion was a chance meeting and you were busy canvassing somewhere in East Ward. We exchanged greetings, shook hands, and went our respective ways.

Yet there is a piece of unfinished business between us, and I would like to see the end of it, for these last few months I have been going to so many memorial and funeral services that I begin to wonder how much longer one has got before becoming one of the great majority oneself, and also because what I have to say may just be of interest to you.

When I stood down in 1971 after five years as Leader or Chairman of the Conservative Group I represented Aldingbourne: the Group wished to honour me in some way (at least, I think that was what was behind it) and thus I became one of the shortest serving aldermen in the history of the aldermanic system. Also, I think uniquely, as aldermen were to be abolished and it was presumably considered not worth holding an election for the period remaining in the life of the county, I remained as county councillor for Aldingbourne. Roy Dunlop who I hear died only last week, lived in Aldingbourne but represented Warbington, said he wanted to stand for Aldingbourne which technically, as I was on the Aldermanic Bench, I had surrendered. Had I wished to fight Roy for the nomination [for the completely new county council], I believe I would have little difficulty in getting the nomination, as the population centre (i.e. where the votes are) was Shripney and Bersted - assuming he would have had the support of the Aldingbourne branch. As he lived there, and I did not, it seemed to me that he had a good claim to the seat and I offered no contest. I suppose because I was past Constituency chairman, then still SE Area [Local Government] chairman, and past Leader, all sorts of county divisions in the county wanted me as their candidate. Partly this was due to all the publicity the Party was putting round at that time: a new County Council was to be born; make sure you are well satisfied with your councillor - he does not have a freehold on the seat. As chairman of SE Area [L.G.] I was at that time addressing meetings all over the place saying just this - it was the party line, and not even my worst enemy would claim I was ever other than a Party man!

Ronnie Shields [Major-General] was as you know Branch chairman of East Ward at the time, and was elected to serve on the S.E. council of which I was also a member. We would travel together to the meetings in London and he asked me - for the first time (I think in the June before the elections the following year) whether I would stand for Chichester East - an invitation he repeated on at least four occasions. On each occasion, I asked about you, particularly whether you had been told. He said that you belonged to the agricultural side of the county, and were not really interested in the city, but that in any event, the branch wanted me. On each occasion, I said that if the branch really wanted me, he (that is yourself) had to be informed - to give you the chance of finding another seat if you wanted one. There were three divisions in the Bognor area that had asked me to be their candidate, but Shields had asked me first and in effect I had pledged myself to him (and as I thought, to East Ward - a ward where I had had my offices since 1946 and which I knew intimately, so therefore it seemed appropriate). Never at any time did I broach the subject of the candidature to Ronnie Shields - he was the one to introduce it to me. He is now dead, but as he was a former Army man I have no doubt he was an honourable man, and if he were alive today he would agree with my version of the facts.

The selection meeting was, as you will recall, left until the very last minute, and I was getting increasingly anxious because everywhere else had had their meetings and there seemed to be such an unbusinesslike feeling towards it; literally, at the very last moment, he asked me if I would stand in South Ward (Pope was the member of the former council and was standing for the new one as an Independent). There was no organization there; I had not been asked by anyone in South Ward, and I refused, but Ronnie said that was all right, he still wanted me for East Ward.

It was at this moment that things began to happen. Buckle [now 1971, Leader of Conservative Group] phoned me on the Sunday morning, using language which in those days as indeed, by my standards today, would rank as obscene, asking (I will leave out the expletives) what I was doing, standing against you as he had plans for you in the new Council. On the Monday, Conservative Central Office was telephoned by him, and Lady Silverstone (as she then was) [Chairman, South Eastern Area] telephoned me to say that he was accusing me of using undue influence as chairman of SE Area LG, to get your seat. Of course, I had not even mentioned SE Area and it would not have cut any ice if I had, as she well knew. The rest of that time up to the Selection Meeting consisted of Roth writing me a letter which I still have telling me to stand down and of the chairman of Singleton - a branch I more than anyone as divisional chairman, had been responsible for forming - telling Oughton the agent that if I were selected against you he would make sure Chichester Division would never get another halfpenny from his branch. Then finally, on the afternoon, I got a call from

Oughton who told me to keep away from the Churchill Room because this would avoid a confrontation with you, since you would refuse to allow me in the room, or something of that sort, until you had addressed them.

All this is ancient history; Roy is now dead; Shields is now dead; Oughton is now dead, Lady Silverstone is now dead, and I do not know what has happened to the remaining players in this affair which itself should be dead and safely buried - but when I received Oughton's call that afternoon and accordingly withdrew, I have had not a single word of apology from anyone or of explanation - which is fair enough and I do not complain. But I would like to set the record straight with you, who I believe had no idea of the background to my involvement (or rather, non-involvement) with East Ward all those years ago. Had I tried to undermine your position, I would have deserved your contempt, and for all I know, you may have thought this is what I attempted to do.

I hope you don't mind me writing you - but I have felt I would like to get all this off my chest and it is just possible, you might still be interested. Don't trouble to reply.

Hope things are going well with you and yours, and that perhaps one day we may meet again.

Yours very sincerely

Barry Rose

PS: On reading this through, I should say in fairness to Ronnie that at the very end, when he suggested I should go to South Ward, and I declined, he asked <u>me</u> to let you know! I said this was his job - I wouldn't have minded so much the previous year, when there was hope for everyone to get a seat, but at that late stage it would have been impossible, but I suppose he had put off telling you so long that in the end, he wanted me to break the ice. I am sure it wasn't my job at any time, but especially not on the stated eve of the adoption meeting!

David Blacker

David did not reply to my letter; instead, he 'phoned and suggested we met at the (old) Dolphin and Anchor. Unfortunately he died in, (I think) the latter part of 2002, but at our meeting we were both agreed that Shields, good soldier he may have been, in political terms he was just not 'with it'.

As for Stanley Roth and Ernest Oughten, the Agent - naturally, my memory goes back a fairly long way - to Harry Ablewhite, both pre- and post-1945 - Agent for the Constituency - who, when seats were falling like ninepins elsewhere, was actually able to increase the majority for the then sitting Member, L.W. Joynson-Hicks. Subsequently, I learned that the two fell out and Ablewhite was retired early, as a result of skull-duggery following his discovery that Joynson-Hicks had been putting out feelers for a neighbouring constituency, whose agent had tipped off Ablewhite. It is a tough old world for agents! It may seem I am straying somewhat from my letter to Blacker - but it ties in when I say that at this time Roth was vice-chairman of the Association and I was involved myself in some skull-duggery for the Association by Gerald Acton who succeeded Ablewhite as Agent. Acton, too, was a good Agent who inherited considerable problems in the Constituency (in those days it was truly huge - from Worthing on the east to the border with Hampshire on the west, to Horsham on the north and including towns such as Midhurst and Petworth and Pulborough and Arundel, as well as Bognor and Littlehampton). One of the first problems he faced was the election of a new Association chairman, and Roth as vice-chairman was naturally the front runner. (I believe he was also chairman of the Bench at the time, and a member of the county council.) To put it bluntly, it was made my job to arrange he did not get the chairmanship of the Association. At the meeting I heard the retiring chairman, Douglas Scriven, make a truly devastating attack on his vice-chairman and his reasons for not proposing Roth to succeed him - Walter (Bill) Loveys won the election for the chairmanship instead. My own part in the drama was, I suspect, leaked, and I would say that Roth never forgave me, although he was reasonably amicable for the last 10-15 years or so of his life. He was my 'business landlord' for many years, which could have created difficulties. A complicated man - badly injured during the war - he richly deserves a book devoted wholly to himself, rather than a few lines here.

However, almost immediately following those association-shattering events, Joynson-Hicks (on the death of his brother) was elevated to the House of Lords, and Walter (Bill) Loveys became the Member. Gerry Acton moved on, and John Pitt became Agent. Bill Loveys asked me to become chairman (following Commander Ashton who had been vice-chairman to Bill, someone incidentally who had been No. 2 target of the Stern Gang in the Palestine conflict; he told me he had to race up the gangplank to get to his ship each night before some terrorist marksman had drawn a bead on him). By this time we had had boundary redistribution but even so, I recall when I ended my stint as chairman, we still had 39 branches or other organisations serving over 13,000 members. Then John died, so I had to become Acting Agent for quite a few months until his successor, Patrick Doherty, was appointed, but whose stay (if eventful) was short; he went North as Area Agent. By this time I had ended my eighth year as association chairman, so

I think I knew a little about Agents and their importance and their responsibilities - but to be frank, I still have my no idea why Oughten in effect so unnecessarily banned me from the Committee Room when the selection was due to take place - I had received no invitation from Shields, so I had no intention of going anyway. But to be charitable to Oughten, his chairman for East Ward was Shields, who I suspect might have had just sort of glimmering of what a mess he had made of things, and thought this the best way of getting out of it - Alex Sayer, who died in 2003, heard about it, offered to stand down in my favour for Pagham, but of course this was completely unacceptable to me as he had already been selected by the Pagham branch.

As it happened, I never had an opportunity of discussing Blacker's contribution to the Conservative Group and County Hall, but by chance, much later, I met him outside my offices in Chichester, when he told me he had fought the previous General Election as a U.K. Independence Party candidate, and had done very well.

To return to David Blacker's election to the County Council - Lt. Col. Ranson was chairman of Singleton Branch, which I suppose as much as anyone, I formed myself with the aid of Sir Rex Benson, at his house in Singleton (to be precise, in his billiards' room). I have not the remotest idea how I upset Ranson - I remember some time later I found myself in a small luncheon party where he also was a guest, I confess I was just a little cool, but what else can a chap do?

Buckle himself: Ah yes. Another time, perhaps. (Suffice to say, at this stage, that the 'Clandestine' meeting so called, was in my office, and as chronicled in the purported 'history'). See Appendix III *ante*, the letter to John Hooley.

APPENDIX V:

I stood in the same election as an Alternative Conservative against Edward Heath. For me, it all began oddly enough at a reception of the Society of Conservative Lawyers; it was at the old Nat. West Headquarters (then I believe one of the tallest buildings in London, and before the I.R.A. bombing). Coming down from the roof, where on a clear day it was said you could see eight counties, I heard a fellow member, whom I did not know, say, "I'm going to oppose Heath." I butted in and said humorously, "Oh no, you're not. I am going to oppose Heath." We had a few friendly words, and, as he was younger than myself, I said I would help him. We left it like that - then I perceived he was not standing after all, so I did so. About two years later, I met him at another function, and asked him why he had not stood. He told me the Chairman of the Carlton Club (Willie Whitelaw) had said to him if he went ahead, he would see to it he was expelled, as Ted was a friend of his! Anyway, I went ahead, although of course I knew I hadn't a chance. Although I was offered help from my 'home' constituency, I was determined not to take away anybody from *that* constituency - although one of my friends, Terence Pickering, helped enormously, and another, Dickie Austen, volunteered £500 to help with my expenses, but alas died before the Election. But neither were Party 'activists', so I never felt I was robbing my 'home' constituency of any of its workers. And there was one other person, whom I didn't know, in Old Bexley, who sent £10 to help - for which I was grateful. Others, in Old Bexley, gave generously of their time.

APPENDIX VI:

I was at an annual conference of one of the local government associations, and as I listened to the debates, I could see that little was 'getting through' to the *elected* members, as opposed to the permanent officials. It struck me that local government needed an association for *elected* members - from my brief experiences, the training that newly elected members was minimal - something like, "If I were you, I'd keep quiet for the first year or so, and listen."

For the vast sums of money spent by local authorities over the wide range of services, it seemed to be not enough. What was needed was that members should have available the 'experts' in relation to their subject - say, housing, public health, planning or whatever as subjects - and to have a weekend course in a decent but not wildly expensive hotel, and for the meetings to be on a completely impartial party political basis.

I was then, I suppose, in addition to a lot of other things, involved in local government from the official side - perhaps I could explain, because I fear few people nowadays either never knew or have forgotten that until well into the 19th century, local government was administered by Justices of the Peace. Thus, the journal over which I presided was called *Justice of the Peace and Local Government Review* (actually, it had a much longer title in 1837 when it was founded, but we need not go into that, except to say that quite obviously, from a very young age, I began to know a fair amount about local government, being in receipt of government reports, official circulars, press releases and so on, quite apart from the articles submitted and accepted).

There seemed absolutely no form of training given on a regular basis, and it struck me that this should be remedied.

I invited Herbert Brabin, the Conservative Party Local Government Officer, and G.W. Reynolds, the Labour Local

Government Officer, to lunch with me at Simpsons, where we discussed the problem, and as I understood the matter, all three of us were united in expressing agreement with my view. I hired (and less there be any suspicion of waste of public money, paid for myself) the Kingsway Hall, and sent round a circular to the mayors and chairman of all councils in England and Wales. I timed the meeting for 23rd April - I deliberately chose St. George's Day (stupid Pooterish me!) as I knew there would be many battles ahead. By this time, Reynolds had became a Labour M.P., and Brabin seemed to be luke-warm, so in order that it should remain non-party political, I suggested that Bill Loveys should be the Conservative Chairman and Reynolds the Labour Party chairman. We recruited the services of Jimmy Elder as Honorary Secretary (a friend of mine, employed as Deputy Secretary by the Rural District Councils Association) and we wrote to the Nuffield Trust for financial assistance. They promised us £4,000, to be spent in four areas, but before handing it over they discussed it with the Permanent Secretary at the Ministry of Housing and Local Government (the formidable Dame Evelyn Sharp) who used her influence to cut the grant to £1,000, and with the instruction it had to be spent on courses in the West Riding.

Of course, the money was minimal - but the grant from the Nuffield Trust had the great advantage that it gave the association "respectability" - and we were up and running. The difference between the Association and individual councils was that say, we would not have a treasurer addressing his own members with consequent possible embarrassment; he might be invited to speak 100 miles away, to make possibly the same speech but the members were able to measure their own experience against those of other councils. They were not *his* members; he was not *their* official - so ideas could easily flow. Both members and officers seemed to find it an exhilarating experience; also, in the evening, an exchange of views could be discussed in a friendly atmosphere.

Of course, "the powers that be" ultimately saw the value of courses, and the Local Government Association has got into the act. But somewhat naturally, I still think the Association of Councillors did it best. Without doubt, the early and unexpected deaths of Bill Loveys and Gerry Reynolds within months of each other - in removing two with the status of M.P. as joint chairmen and also as keen "local government" men, was a loss indeed for the Association. The new secretary decided to become M.P. for Gateshead, and we were back again in square one. (The Liberal Party (as it then was) saw what we were doing, and founded its own Association for Liberal councillors.) I served as President for many years, but I suspect local government reforms have not been kind to it. However, the last I heard (for the Association was long since removed my name from its mailing list) they had changed the name from the Association of Councillors, to the *National* Association of Councillors (which I am sure made a very great difference). I hope they are still adhering to the original principles - because I think it really performed a needed and worth-while function. Personally, I always thought it needed a former (retired) chief officer to be C.E.O. - a man or woman in mid-fifties or early sixties, would in my opinion, be the answer.

But this explanatory note explains the various references to the Association in this book.

APPENDIX VII:

AS OTHERS SEE US ...

The following, written by one of our Authors, W.B. Podevin, came unsolicited a month or so after a visit (with a co-author) to discuss their book.

Imagine, if you will, a medieval market town close adjacent to the south coast of England, now much modernised in its outer extremities but still retaining much of its Roman brick and cobblestone walls. The narrow streets within the boundary of the old town nestle together for support and company, little seems to have been constructed since the end of the eighteenth century except to replace those crumbling edifices erected in even earlier days. The office to which we were bound was situated amid the warren of streets and lanes in the north east quadrant of the town, in a converted warehouse of uncertain age or provenance, so much refurbished over the years as to now little reflect the desire or intention of its original creator.

A ring on the bell, a footstep within, the door opened by a casually dressed young man. Having satisfied his inquiry as to our business with the establishment, we were ushered briefly to a book-lined waiting room and shortly conducted up five flights of stairs to the inner sanctum of the gentleman we had travelled to see that morning.

The sanctum revealed much of the character of its occupant. Piles of paper, files, magazines, books and other office paraphernalia covered every surface of the room, from desk to bookcase to chair to windowsill and back again via the umbrella stand, sideboard and easy chairs. No surface was innocent of a paper of some description. Whether this friendly clutter was to reflect upon the normal state of mind of the man, who, arising from his station behind the desk to greet us warmly, I knew not.

He shook our hands while his minion cleared the impedimenta from two chairs, bade us be seated and inquired after our journey, while we, indulging in the small talk befitting the preliminaries of our meeting, took in our surroundings and its owner. Our host was a chubby, almost angelically faced man of middle height, in his early sixties as near as I could judge, well dressed in a formal suit, a plain shirt and [club] tie, and having a warm friendly manner about him which presaged well for our mutual interest.

We began the discussion of our business and after ten or so minutes thus engaged, our host raised his hand in horror. "I am so remiss," he explained in apparent confusion. "You have been here ten minutes at least after your long journey and I haven't yet offered you any refreshment. Do please have a glass of champagne." He seemed quite upset that we declined his kind offer but was soon mollified when it was determined that we would accept his invitation to luncheon.

A few minutes later we were again ushered down the five flights of stairs towards the street and a superb trattoria nearby. Our host led the way after assuming his velvet-collared overcoat and, to our great surprise, a billycock hat, its well-brushed brown fur shining in the sunlight. That hat, it could only have been procured from Locks of St. James's. My partner and I reached a simultaneous conclusion. Our host just had to be Mr. Pickwick or his reincarnation. He could be no other.

[I sometimes wear a billycock hat when in Chichester, but of course never in London. He was right however, about it being from Lock's.]